HOW TO AVOID
BURGLARY,
HOUSEBREAKING
AND OTHER CRIMES

All statements made and opinions given
in this book are, unless otherwise
specified, those of the author.

Second printing before publication, September, 1967
Third printing, December, 1967

© 1967, by Ulrich Kaufmann
Library of Congress Catalog Card Number: 67–27033
PRINTED IN THE UNITED STATES OF AMERICA

How to Avoid Burglary, Housebreaking and Other Crimes

by Ulrich Kaufmann

CROWN PUBLISHERS, INC., NEW YORK

TO MY WIFE

CONTENTS

HOW TO AVOID BURGLARY, HOUSEBREAKING AND OTHER CRIMES

FOREWORD

Security is more than a lock on the door.

This book was in the planning stage for over ten years. It was not prepared because the author enjoys writing, but because the longer he traveled, lived, and researched, the more he realized the urgent need to get some effective down-to-earth information into the hands of the millions of potential victims of smart criminals.

The "bad guys" can start their training (which at times is excellent) at the corner hangout or join group instruction on the empty lot down the street. For postgraduate courses they can attend the many fine bull sessions in any respectably large jail; and even some of the smaller jails and reformatories now have inmates who can offer excellent suggestions in specialized fields. In most cases, the faculty of inmates teaches a foundation sufficient for the newcomer to go into the world and start on his own.

The "good guys," on the other hand, can have discussions with neighbors who, nine times out of ten, know as little about fighting crime as the person who asks the questions. Now there are schools, universities, and libraries available to almost everyone, and it is relatively simple to get detailed information about (plus a good definition of) burglary, robbery, and any other type of crime, all with Latin names, technical terms, and possibly detailed descriptions in layman's language. Lawbooks give information concerning the exact punishment prescribed for each crime, psychology books give an insight into the innermost motivation for our various types of criminals—but when nice John Doe has all this information, *what is he going to do about it?* How will all this newfound knowledge help him to stop the crime that may be planned against him at this very moment?

To quote punishment tables to the intruder who stands over your bed at two o'clock in the morning will scarcely be effective. Nor will explaining that the reason he now stands there is because he hated his father while still attending kindergarten. But what *will* help?

Outsmarting smart criminals is no easy task. It requires solid planning and careful habits. Most of us are in the market for a fire extinguisher one day after our house burns down; we shop for a snow shovel only after we are completely snowed in. The time to start protecting yourself is now.

But perhaps you live in one of those Utopias where everything is wide open, nothing secured, because everybody is honest, and nothing has ever been stolen. You should still be on the alert. J. Edgar Hoover recently reported that arrests for burglary alone have *increased in a single year* at the following rates:

Rural	9.0%
Suburban	8.3%
City	9.7% for males
	22.6% for females (!)

Sooner or later your Utopia will be invaded, too. Burglars already visit the rest of us at the unbelievable rate of once every twenty-eight *seconds*.

No matter how many courses you may study, no matter how many books you may read, we all know there is no sure cure for all the ills and crimes in this world, and no assurance that all unpleasantries with the criminal element in society can be avoided. It is not the business of this book to try to solve all of these problems. *How to Avoid Burglary, Housebreaking and Other Crimes* is designed, quite simply, to help you prepare your defenses, to help you protect your home, your possessions, your loved ones, and your very life—*without* spending money unnecessarily and *without* taking unnecessary chances.

-1-

Outside the Home

The most important lesson learned by the writer in a long career of service with United States Government security services was: *Put yourself in the shoes of the criminal before you attempt to understand him, catch him, or defend yourself against him.*

The person who has designs on your home—to enter, break in, or steal—does not start with the third shelf down in your linen closet to look for valuables. He has to get there first. Put yourself in his shoes, and take a walk down to the end of your block and back again. Walk slowly and see your block through the eyes of a person who will break into one of these houses before the milkman makes his rounds the next morning. Try to find a likely target, more promising than all the others. You must consider:

1. Ease of entry
2. Possibility of detection
3. Chances of getting caught
4. Size of possible loot
5. Net profit per year in jail.

Since most of the above information is not readily available to the man in the street, one of your objects should be to keep this information from marauders.

Avenues of Approach

You say a window is a window is a window, and a front door is a front door is a front door. Not so to Adolf, the villain, who plans to visit without detection from owner, neighbor, or police. (And he does not underestimate the powers of observation of our neighborhood kids, who can be quite successful in nailing him before he reaches first base.) Before Adolf can search that linen closet, he must get into the house. His object is to find a weak point for entry.

Cover for concealment was a nice thing to find when you played hide-and-go-seek, and it is invaluable for a soldier fighting in battle; it is no less effective for Adolf. Why should he take chances crossing a long open front yard when there is one house with a beautiful thick hedge running the entire length of the property? Why should he approach the house directly behind that powerful streetlamp when the third one down is in complete darkness? Why set foot on a piece of ground where a vicious-looking dog sits in the window, or a small yippy dog is so noisy that it can be heard down to the end of the street?

The chances are that any Adolf in any locale will use existing openings. Although front or back door are your friends' first choices, Adolf never planned to become a friend of yours. Hence, any opening from basement window to upstairs bathroom may suit his purpose. This includes that vent opening at the far side of your house, the one you could have sworn was too small for a child to get through.

Why pick an exposed window facing the street, when foundation planting offers cover for another very nicely? Why indeed would Adolf want to start working on the window, which can be seen from your neighbor's bedroom, when the opposite side of the house cannot be observed from that windowless garage of the Browns?

The upstairs window is more difficult to enter. And who wants to lug a ladder down the street, especially at night? But have you noticed how that lovely tree right along Dr. Livingston's house has grown? If you were a small boy you'd have fun climbing among the handy branches; Adolf has his eyes on it for different reasons.

Take an Educated Guess

All right, one home may offer more protection against entry than the other, but what about the loot? At best, the value of possessions inside a house is difficult to determine from the street. Two cars in the driveway don't exactly indicate a poverty-stricken family. But one glance is not enough. A diving board for a built-in swimming pool prominently exposed out in the back yard (while the neighbor's kids run through the sprinklers to cool off); a large compressor unit next to the home for house air conditioning (while the Browns next door use a 10-inch oscillating fan in the window); expensive children's toys rusting away in the yard because nobody cares (while Karen across the street has to struggle along on last year's bike); and many, many other indications, like a 60-foot antenna in addition to several other modern TV and FM antennas, electrically operated garage doors, an underground sprinkler, plus that collection of priceless (?) *objets d'art* prominently displayed in several windows facing the street, all help to indicate the amount of loot available inside.

If *everybody* in the block has most of the above items then, of course, they fail to be signals for tonight's target. Adolf will then shop for that four-car garage, the big fountain on a manicured lawn, or the two tennis courts in the back. *Nobody* has those items previously mentioned? Then the gleam may come to his eye when he finds the only garage on the block, or the only lawn which shows evidence that the owner could afford to spend a five-dollar bill on a bag of fertilizer.

Clearly, your home is not as well guarded as Fort Knox, and the chances of getting in are much greater. But what about this unknown factor of profit once a person succeeds in entering? The secret formula of dividing loot by number of years in jail times chances of getting caught is still being worked out on the "hot line" between Sing Sing and that big wheel of fortune. Even if this formula is ever perfected, make your home the least likely target for tonight!

What You Can Do

If the burglar's approach to your home looks different to you now, *please, whatever you do, don't start moving, don't cut any trees or hedges, and don't get excited.* You needn't cut that "staircase" of a tree, leading right up to the second-story bedroom window. Remember that thousands of windows face permanent outside fire escapes. Your tree is by no means a greater hazard than a fire escape—and it's so much prettier! It simply requires that you check window security a bit more closely.

Do you have a thick hedge or other growth that offers concealment between street and house? Stick a larger light bulb into your front door fixture, and cut those few small branches right next to this light, since they reduce efficiency immensely. Consider adding a light at the other end of the house, possibly a spotlight which would throw its beam across the entire front. If you want to save electricity, you don't have to leave lights on all night, but do have them mounted prominently so Adolf will know they are there. Want to splurge? Have a switch for the outside lights next to your bed. Then, even if you only think there was a noise outside, you can flip them on for a few minutes.

The more lights you can afford, the better off you'll be. Note that no matter how powerful or unobstructed the front and back door lights may be, the sides of your home remain dark. In most cases two additional regular or spotlights, placed properly, can illuminate the perimeter efficiently with a minimum amount of fixtures.

You don't live in a box-shaped house? Then draw the outline of your home in the center of a piece of paper, stick a pin into a likely place for number one light, and run straight lines or a thread (the beams of light) past your outline. Upon discovering a shaded area, either move the pin to a more advantageous location or consider investment in one or two additional lights along that wall. Go to location number two, and continue until you have covered all areas to your satisfaction. Better still, take an extension cord, and after nightfall actually experiment with your particular situation.

Pay particular attention to any extensions or protrusions along any of your outside walls. Mounting an additional light on the west side of your chimney may leave a vulnerable ground-floor window in complete darkness, while mounting this same light toward the east will light this area well, leaving only a windowless wall in darkness.

Please note carefully that all suggested locations are alongside or near your house. At no time allow yourself to be talked into following the builder's plan of illuminating his model home with spotlights directed at the model. He wants only to attract attention to increase his sales, while you and I are interested in security. You may want to borrow some of his ideas for bringing out the best points of your residence during a garden party, but: *Please use separate switches for show-off lights and your security lights.*

The reason is simple. Not only Adolf, but all his friends and relatives can safely gather behind any of these show-off lights with the full knowledge that they cannot be spotted from any of your windows, since *you will be the one who is blinded* by your very own lights. When security lights go on, *he* is the one who is illuminated.

*Note how two sides of your home remain dark
with present outside lights.*

Unless you have a particular love for bright lights, it will not be necessary to run an electric cable behind each tree, shrub or bush. Though one bush may be so dense that it is virtually impossible to detect anyone in it or behind it, the important fact is that the bush is illuminated. Adolf knows the bush is illuminated when he stands there while the lights go on, but he will never know whether you detected his white socks or any other part of him. (If you were Adolf, would you wait around to find out?)

At this very moment Adolf also remembers from his training days that the owner of the property does not have to wait to call police until a strange hand is found in the linen closet, or a stranger is found walking inside the home. That foot behind the bush is already ripe for charges of trespassing and prowling, without proving intent.

If for some reason you do not want to run additional wires for new lights on the outside of your home, purchase a reliable and powerful battery-operated flashlight. At night take this light and "scan" your property from inside the house, get to know what it looks like without any undesirables hiding. Notice that dead branch at the bottom of your corner bush, which is *not* anyone's foot; observe the light-colored bark on one of the trees, which is *not* a human face. While observing

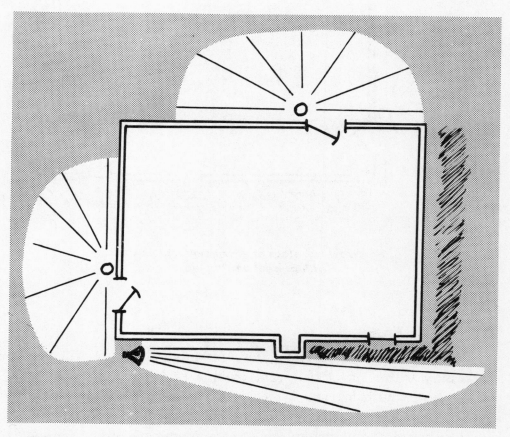

Watch for an obstruction, like a chimney, when mounting additional lights.

through a closed window, place the light right up against the window-pane, and shield it with your free hand; this will prevent any reflection from blurring your vision.

Yours is the house right behind the streetlamp? Yes. this light is a good deterrent, but watch for the night when this lamp is not lit. If you happen to see the boys hit it with a rock while playing, well and good. If you do not know the reason for its failure, and are the cautious type, you might suspect Adolf's little BB gun (for which he needs no license). For some reason he may have picked your home despite the lamp, and during his reconnaissance walk eliminated one of your protective devices. Don't panic, just go over the checklist at the end of this book a bit more carefully, and notify the utility company of the streetlight's location.

Dogs

That dog of yours does not have to be a school-trained, hundred-pound-plus, man-attacking beast. The fact that he is there, that he has a voice, and that he uses that voice when strangers approach the house is effective. Don't inform any and all strangers at your door that he is the sweetest thing who would not harm a fly; don't brag about your sleeping so soundly that no amount of barking or other noise will ever awaken you. It's all part of the guessing or intelligence game which does not feed information to the opposition on a silver platter. Adolf will be awake when visiting. How does he know that the timid bark of this twelve-pound, four-legged weakling did not set off a chain reaction which will have a squad car on his neck within minutes?

You don't have a dog? Why not get your youngsters one? They have wanted one anyway all along, and here you have an additional justification for his existence. To keep Adolf from selecting your home as target, this pooch needs no pedigree.

And where should you keep this dog? I strongly urge that you normally keep him inside the building he is supposed to protect. Especially at night, keep him inside, and give him the free run of the house, if at all possible. To keep him outside on a chain means that he cannot attack any intruder who stays beyond his reach. If he remains loose inside the fence around your property, a rag drenched with the scent of a female in heat at one corner of the estate will hold his undivided attention much longer than it will take Adolf to enter and leave your home from the other side. By either method your dog is exposed to poisoning attempts and to the hypodermic, which can be fired from some distance away.

In an apartment, the dog will probably be right there with you at all times. Your only concern might be that stranger who tries to befriend your dog while you take him for his constitutional. Don't be too concerned. It is amazing how a dog can enjoy attention from a stranger in the street, and only moments later consider this same person his mortal enemy, providing the dog is back in his own "empire," and the stranger attempts to enter.

As with the streetlight that is not functioning on a certain night, use added caution when for some unknown reason faithful Rover is not present or accounted for at the time you are ready to go to bed.

Wealth, Anyone?

As for the outward signs of your affluence, must you give away those *objets d'art* you have been collecting? Tear out the air conditioning? Fill the pool with soil? Let the lawn go to pot? All this just because someone told you it would be safer that way? Hardly. Of course you want to keep all your possessions. But why advertise the fact that you own them. What you may not realize is this: *If enough is prominently on display, a relatively innocent Tom, Dick, or Harry may be jealous enough to try his luck, and make your home his first attempt at burglary.*

The law in your state requires a fence of certain height around your pool? This will hide much in itself, even if the fence is only wire with evergreen shrubs alongside. The casual passerby really can't be sure whether that fence is there to keep your pets from running away, or serves some other purpose. A diving board is different. If you have not chosen a location for the pool, consider placing the deep diving end as far away from the street as is feasible. Before ordering any sky-high diving board, make certain you are placing this order not to impress friends and neighbors, but because at least one member of the family is brave enough to make use of it. Is your diving tower already in place? Take a look from the street, and see if there is not one spot, possibly two, where a tall bush or evergreen will just about hide those steps to the sky.

While you are at the nursery for evergreens, pick up a few for that large box which does not do a particularly good job of hiding a compressor for 123,000 BTU air conditioning.

Your antiques, pictures, *objets d'art* of all descriptions were in all probability purchased for some good reason, and you don't feel like hiding or locking away any of them. You put them where they are now because that is the very spot that brings out the best points in each.

But are the most valuable pieces:

1. Located on the windowsill facing the street?

2. Fastened to the window frame on that same window?

3. On a narrow shelf in window, so more can be displayed?

4. On a table directly behind this window?

5. And that biggest, most valuable painting on the opposite wall, with a museum-type lamp mounted just above it, to make certain that the artist's name can be read at night even from outside?

The author will make every attempt to remain diplomatic and not ask the obvious question; but our friend Adolf would ask you point blank: Is every one of your lovely pieces of art in its present place because it really looks best where it is, or did you stage this display to make certain that none of the neighbors will overlook a single sign of your wealth?

No, don't hide them all. But do consider the possibility of moving some, and do consider keeping those light curtains closed at all times, and closing the drapes when the lights go on. Shutters? Venetian blinds? Shades? All are fine if they will serve the purpose. Go outside yourself, and see how many of your fine possessions are visible; do it both during the daytime and nighttime, with your curtains open and closed, with the lights on and off.

Make sure that there are no expensive toys rusting away on your front lawn, so that Adolf will not conclude: (1) that the family is wealthy, (2) that Junior is careless and negligent, and (3) that careless and negligent rich children often enough have careless and negligent rich parents.

The moral? Use camouflage and care if you want to keep all those fine possessions. Remember: A burglary occurs once very twenty-eight seconds!

-2-

Outside Your Apartment

No crabgrass to fight. No leaves to rake. No grass to cut. After reading the preceding pages, you may also be glad of what seems to be much better security from criminals. To a certain degree you do have fewer vulnerable points where a burglar or intruder can strike, but that still leaves an Achilles' heel or two to guard.

Anything outside of your own apartment falls under your landlord's jurisdiction, and many of his actions will be dictated by building codes, fire regulations, local ground rules—and his budget. But before going to him with big and expensive ideas for airtight security or recommendations for sweeping changes in his present security setup, *put yourself in the criminal's shoes* again.

Walk carefully from the street to your apartment door. Before reaching the door, notice whether there are steps outside the house that cast shadows in corners below. Is the front door open? Does it stay open most of the time? Too bad—it could be a good checkpoint to keep out undesirables. Is there a more or less impressive but dimly lit entrance hall with heavy curtains, furniture to hide behind or even under? An adjoining room with mailboxes, coke machine, and a telephone booth far enough from the wall to hide any seven-footer who weighs under two hundred and fifty pounds? A few extra lights will help lessen these hazards.

You have a doorman? Wonderful. He can be a great deterrent to unwanted visitors through the *main* entrance. Of particular value is the doorman who is not sound asleep in the basement or who does not read yesterday's comics out of sight of his assigned duty station.

The Front Door

Of course it is a good idea to keep this portal locked at all times. Keeping it locked is more inconvenient for all concerned, but it is also a lot safer. Your landlord is against locking it? He even had the lock removed? Someone should try to find out why. Most landlords are human beings, somewhat like you and me, and they are anxious to run a secure and safe apartment dwelling. But how often was the super awakened after midnight by the third-floor tenant who had forgotten her key? How often does the landlord have to have his front door repaired because certain tenants are rough or impatient.

Before you start storming into the renting office demanding a bigger, better, more secure front door, you'd better check with a few tenants, and find out if they are willing to play the game according to civilized rules. And while speaking to other occupants, you might want to point out that the lights in and around the building are placed there for a reason, not to serve as a supply point for people needing bulbs. The variety store on the corner sells bulbs at a more or less reasonable price.

Why You?

But why should you be the one to take the trouble of talking to fellow tenants? Especially in places like New York City, where thousands of believable jokes are based on the fact that Apartment 3B knows nothing whatever about the occupants of 3C, does not care, and, further, may want to keep it that way. Nobody asks you to become a busybody who makes a full-time profession out of prying into other people's business. However, you may want to consider this: *Any chain is as strong as its weakest link.*

In a private home, father, mother, and fourteen of their children can be as security-conscious as is humanly possible. All do just the right thing morning, noon, and night. A secure home? Their fifteenth child cares nothing about home, family, or security. When coming home after everyone is asleep he sometimes closes the front door properly, sometimes not; he never locks it. All security measures are nullified because of carelessness on the part of *one* individual in a private home. The story is no different in any multiple dwelling; it's just that the problem is magnified.

You feel it might be a worthwhile undertaking to sell fellow occupants on security? That careless boy who never locks doors may resent any further admonitions from Dad, but he might be willing to listen more readily to advice from fellow teenagers or even a brother. By the same token the tenant in apartment 3C may already have called the landlord a dictator, and will greatly resent any further proclamations emanating from his headquarters, without ever reading them or trying to understand the reason for them. But you—you suave diplomat—how can she resist your approach as a fellow tenant who has only the best interest of each occupant at heart?

Seriously, unless we live by ourselves on a lonely island, much of our physical security, especially while at home, depends on the actions of our fellow occupants. Just as we would assist one another in case of fire, why not pull together in security matters?

An intercom is of no value if, when the bell rings in apartment 3C, the front-door release latch is automatically activated by a tenant too busy to find out who might be at the door downstairs. Even you could be misusing this simple security device on the afternoon a visitor is expected, because you answer the bell with an automatic buzz, without waiting for a reply on the intercom.

What about educating those fine, upstanding citizens who reside at the same address with you, before they start storming out demanding tighter security? Not only should you advise them that the lock in the front door and the intercom *are to be used,* but perhaps they will be willing to contribute a quarter a month, in addition to the already high rent, to support an additional security device. Cooperation and understanding will greatly improve security. Your landlord probably has as much urgent concern over that mugging and those two burglaries as you do—but are they *his* fault or a careless tenant's?

Other Devices

We briefly touched on the two most widely used items designed to discourage unwanted visitors. A complete list of all additional gadgetry would stagger the imagination. A few will be described here; others can be found in Chapter 16.

To begin with, a surveillance camera could be mounted in such a position that the guard, on duty at the central console, could see you leave your cab or approach the building arm in arm with your escort before actually entering the building. Additional cameras could escort you not only through the lobby, but into, as well as inside, the elevator, and the ones located on each floor accompany you every step of the way to your own apartment door.

Instead of, or in addition to these cameras, corridor speakers can be mounted throughout the building. Not the one-way type, but the ones some people refer to as squawk boxes. Very simple: The guard who just saw Miss Jones enter the building can carry on a conversation with her from that moment until she is safely in her own apartment, since these boxes are sensitive enough to pick up Miss Jones's voice while she walks down the hall or rides the elevator. You're not the talkative type? Don't say a word, just go on your way and skip the "good evening" (if you must). Protection is still there, since the guard hears any strange noises throughout the building and, upon hearing anything out of the ordinary, would inquire, "Are you all right, Miss Jones?" If there is no answer, he or his assistant will investigate.

In lieu of these permanent installations, a system of small, inexpensive, short-range two-way radios could be worked out with all tenants.

Any number of alarm devices, similar to fire-alarm boxes, could be placed along this short walk we are taking. The alarm could be connected to the police department, to a guard service, to the doorman right in the building, or to the outside of the building where it would bring Officer Murphy running.

There is hardly a limit to what a good security system can do for you. If the price is right, escort service could be provided from front door to apartment and for an additional few cents the armed and bonded guard could see to it that you are safely tucked in.

To keep our friend Adolf out in the first place, a camera at the locked front door, connected to a receiver in each apartment could supplement the present intercom. The camera would be used not only to look at a visitor's face but also to inspect his credentials, to determine if he really is that man from the telephone company.

If you are the landlord, install a keyless lock; then you can throw away all keys and the lock that goes with them. Each tenant then only has to remember a few numbers to activate the lock. Whenever some-one moves out, or at other times when it is deemed necessary, numbers for a combination lock can be changed. Only tenants and authorized

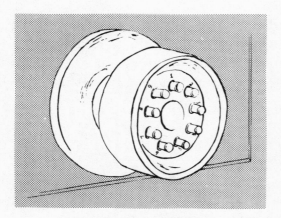 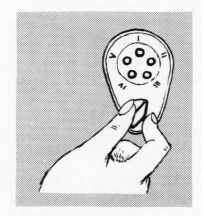

*(Left) Instead of inserting a key, push buttons, then turn knob . . .
or (right) push buttons and turn a small switch to open door.*

 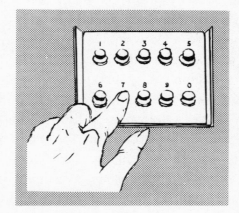

*(Left) You may prefer dialing your way in, then pulling handle to open
door . . . or (right) letting electric current open door,
after you push correct buttons.*

persons would be notified of the new combination. If it is difficult for you to remember numbers, pick any word with the same number of letters as there are digits in the combination. The first letter to appear in the alphabet is number 1 on your combination, second letter is number 2, and so forth. By this method the word LOVE equals 2341 on your lock. And in case you think it is easy to open these locks without knowing the combination, ask your mathematician friend to figure out the number of possibilities. If the astronomical figure does not convince you, then be advised that certain of these locks will automatically block all buttons for several seconds after the incorrect combination has been pushed, convincing any trial and error operator that his attempt is hopeless.

But after this small sample of the wide array of gadgetry available for your safety, consider again the plea made in the preceding pages for working together. Tampering, breaking, misusing, or plain sabotaging these modern, effective devices could endanger everyone.

Security Specialists

That problems exist on both sides of the "Rental Office" sign has been established. But what should be done if the problems are too complicated? There are many reliable security firms throughout the nation who, within a very short period of time, can come up with a long list of specific recommendations based on their analysis of your particular security problems. Your landlord may not like some of the price tags, you may not be able to afford some others; but you may also be amazed at how much protection a single item on the list can offer at a relatively small cost. Not only that, before installing fancy electronic equipment, your specialist may come up with some very fine ideas to implement existing security at no cost to you. For example: You now have a doorman at the building, and each of your tenants has a phone in his apartment. Would it give your tenants a feeling of added security if you let them know that your doorman would come rushing after them to investigate if they had not called him after a reasonable time to report their safe arrival inside their apartment?

This service can be provided regardless of present communications conditions, that is, house phone, switchboard, intercom, or what have

you. For all details and answers to your questions, talk to the local expert. He can suggest that the doorman lock the door before leaving on his investigation trip, or what happens when the line is busy at the time when a tenant wants to report safe arrival (Suggestion: Have the doorman dial the tenant's number at the time of his entry into the building. The tenant will then answer his ringing phone when he arrives safely, while the line cannot be tied up from either end by an outside call).

If you are the landlord, other persons you may want to consult are your own tenants. You think they are all careless, destructive, and couldn't care less what happens to the building? When was the last time you informed them of your plans for improving service and appearance of the place these people call their home? Give it at least a try, state your position, state your plans for possible protection for each one of them, and get their reactions. They really are not stupid, and may come up with some excellent ideas of their own.

The last piece of advice the author can offer is *not to install any device because it looks impressive or costs more than anything you have ever priced before.* Some relatively inexpensive item, properly installed and used, might be just as useful in your particular situation.

Into Bed Without Help

Modern science, electronic devices, and a friendly doorman are fine, *but* you have none of these at your present domicile? But you still desire to get to bed without being molested on your way?

No matter how worried, scared, or late you may be, *do not run.* Running, you are off balance, can't stop or change directions in a hurry; besides, you can't possibly observe everything you may want to avoid in front or alongside of you. You will also draw attention to yourself, which you may not want at this particular time. Walk near the curb where no one can strike you over the head from inside a dark doorway or reach out to pull you into a doorway.

Even as you turn the corner into your own street, follow that relatively safe curb. This way you will not bump face to face into the fellow waiting at the corner building. *Don't ever cut corners anywhere, not on the street, not in hallways, and not when entering your own building.*

Stay away from parked cars, bushes, anything that may hide a

person from your view. Difficult? Then do the best you can by bearing left while danger might be on the right side of the street, and vice versa. Depending on circumstances, width of sidewalk, traffic, and so forth, you may be better off walking in the middle of the street.

Remain "in the gutter" when approaching your house. Anything suspicious? Then *keep on walking past your own address* as though it were only another house on the block. Of course, depending on the situation, you will want to notify the police immediately if there actually is a disturbance or a crime possibly being committed. Don't walk into *your* building to make the call. You may not come out the decorated hero if you tangle singlehanded with an unruly crowd.

Back on the second cruise past your home, and things still don't look right? If there is a member of your family still awake upstairs, phone and request escort service. Or, if you have always gone out of your way to be nice to the super, you may be able to persuade him on the phone to be at the door when you enter the building.

Nobody awake? The police are. They would much rather escort you inside while you can make it under your own power, than carry you out on a stretcher after it is too late. But please don't call that busy desk sergeant every time a piece of paper flies across your front stoop. He will get tired of your crying wolf.

This time all seems quiet and normal as you come in on your final approach. In case the building has a few steps from the street to the front door, you may want to pass just enough to see into the far corner formed by the steps and the outside wall. At any rate, do all your observing from the curb, then walk up the center of the steps. Don't be clever and try to sneak through that passageway to the back entrance because someone told you that the front was too dangerous.

Walk in the center, stay in the center, and don't start investigating or snooping along the way to your own apartment, unless you are looking for trouble. Have you ever thought that somewhere along this walk *you might encounter someone who is much more anxious to hide from you, than you are to avoid him?* It could be nothing more than the kid who stole that fat Sunday paper from in front of Apartment 1B, or it could be the successful criminal who wants to leave the premises undetected. Unless it is absolutely imperative that the mailbox be checked at this hour, or a coke is desperately needed, forego both until tomorrow.

Is there an empty elevator waiting for you? Have a safe ride. Is the elevator waiting with a person you either don't know, or who looks suspicious, or with whom you would just as soon not ride? Then have your good reason for not taking it at this time. If mailboxes are in a well-lit area, you may consider checking for mail. You may walk toward the super's apartment pretending to leave a note in his door, and since this nice fellow is always home, he will come to your rescue in case of need.

If a suspicious person in the elevator gets overly anxious to have your company, and tells you that he will wait, there is still a "No thanks, forgot to buy something for my husband"; and with that you can leave the building again. In case you do have to share this vertical transportation, always stand next to the alarm button. In case of need, *keep pushing* this button although you hear no alarm go off, since you may be activating devices too distant from the elevator to be heard.

At last you made it to your own apartment. Some people believe in ringing their own doorbell either from downstairs or just before entering their abode, the theory being that this will give any possible burglar ample opportunity to escape, and prevent possible violence when he is confronted by the resident. With or without prior warning to intruders, it is never a good idea to rush into dark rooms without reasonable caution.

Before closing and securing that apartment door, let's take one quick look around to determine if there could be an uninvited creature hiding somewhere inside. In case there is, the door is still open for a hasty retreat.

Before You Leave

To make your return into the apartment safer, you may try one or all of the following suggestions *before* departing:

Leave at least one light burning, and you will not have to return to a dark place.

To give yourself a good indication whether someone entered while you were gone, wedge the tip of a toothpick between door and door-jamb, then break off the protruding piece to avoid detection. True, the person who entered and then left again could have replaced this tiny tip of a toothpick (providing he had detected it), but replacement

would be impossible by any person still inside. Caution: Do not use too much force, or the tip may remain "glued" on the doorframe when the door is opened, thus defeating our purpose of having it fall to the ground as a danger signal.

Many people leave lights on, some have used the toothpick trick, but have you ever heard of anyone leaving a radio or TV playing while away? You and I, and Adolf as well, know that no person in his right mind lets that beautiful stereo sound or television picture go to waste with nobody there to enjoy it. Right? So: Why not *leave the set tuned on* at normal volume while absent—to most it will be a sure sign that there is somebody home.

As you give this security business more thought, you will arrive at many good ideas of your own for your particular situation.

replaced? Why does this door get painted only when there is something left in the bucket from another paint job?

Now that we all feel sufficiently sorry for this grossly neglected member of the household, let us take several extra minutes to make it feel wanted. Suppose we begin by pushing it gently from inside and then from the outside, while it remains in a closed position. Does that lower end near the bottom hinge push in quite a bit because three out of three screws are missing? Or does the top half of the door give on the latch side because part of the doorframe and molding are either rotting away or have been removed completely? Or, when pushing in the center, do you get the feeling that the entire locking mechanism may get shoved right out of its recess? Before we go to the actual locking devices, let us take one look at the frame in which this door is mounted. Does it seem rather weak to you? Does it look as though there is an excessive space between door and frame?

The reason we ask these questions is that in a breaking and entering job *Adolf looks to bypass any and all of your locking devices, rather than meet them head on.* It is possible to spread a weak doorframe, thus rendering most ordinary locks ineffective. Let us emphasize this one most important point which holds true for any and all openings, no matter where they are located, no matter how large or small they may be: *No amount of inadequate hardware, mediocre locks, or ordinary devices will secure any opening if the movable part (door, window, etc.) can be moved, pushed, or juggled in its entirety sufficiently away from its encasement to leave bolts and latches holding onto thin air instead of lock strikes or recesses.*

Remember the last time police made an arrest for "possession of burglary tools" and you felt sorry for the suspect, since an ordinary screwdriver was the only evidence? Many other everyday, innocent instruments can be most effective "burglar tools" and we cannot possibly expect law enforcement agencies to confiscate all of them. Suppose that bumper jack were taken out of your automobile, and declared illegal because Adolf could use it in a horizontal position on the very doorframe we are looking at now?

By now you may be firmly convinced that the old saying about locks keeping only honest people out is really true. Don't you believe it! If our government had that defeatist attitude there could be no state secrets. And furthermore, don't feel too guilty about the fact that you own valuables that require protection from "them what don't have." At the other end of the world, Hong Kong, under the worst slum conditions, a hunk of fish will get as much protection as a $10,000 bracelet in the United States. True, the methods vary a bit, but the purpose is the same—and the owner of this piece of yesterday's fish has no qualms about protecting his property with whatever means may be necessary.

It is not suggested that in checking a door or any other openings, tools should be used indiscriminately to force a space between the frame and the opening portion. It is, however, strongly urged that you keep in mind that 1/16th of an inch of present holding power will do no good whatever if a bit of force is applied in the right direction.

In all probability that frame is in good or fair condition, so don't start tearing out woodwork. Even if there is an unusually large space, don't start rebuilding the home. A few wedges from the inside may remedy the situation completely. What we particularly have in mind here are the cellar, garage, and other "neglected" openings where access to framework is easy, since in many cases the builder did not bother to pretty up the surrounding area from the inside. If, for some reason, closing of the gap is not possible or feasible by the application of wedges on the locking side, let's see if adding a full-length strip of wood, securely fastened on the hinge side, will not do the trick. This maneuver entails taking off the door and fastening it again on the newly added lumber, a method not recommended if the space in question is minute.

Neither method may appeal to you if the door leads into a freshly decorated kitchen. In order to place wedges, the existing vertical piece or pieces of molding may have to be removed. If the gap is really large, the other method should be earnestly taken into consideration since it does not have to be noticeable if done properly. If you don't want to go to this trouble, note the appropriate locking devices described in a subsequent chapter.

Certainly you can pick up the phone and order a new door, built to your exact specifications. It's easy, and from a security standpoint there most certainly is no objection.

A new door? Sure, if you have unlimited funds. But the author did not write this book to have you spend money, but rather to make existing items as secure as possible with minimum expenditure. A piece of advice, or a word of caution from these pages, can relocate that impotent hunk of hardware and turn it into a peerless and effective

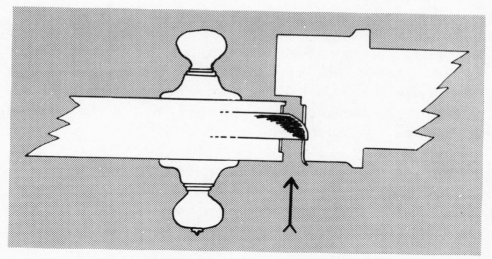

Too much space beween door + frame = danger.

security device. The cost may vary from removal of four screws to a new location, to adding a piece of scrap metal in a strategic place.

At any rate, the amount of money spent on security does not necessarily determine the effectiveness of the system; don't add new doors.

Sealing

While discussing entrances and openings in general, we may mention that it would be foolish to install an expensive device to guard any hardly-ever-used opening. Instead, give consideration to closing it permanently. Before carrying this idea too far, though, first determine that this really is a more or less useless passage to the great outdoors, and further make certain that it does not block your only route of escape in case of fire or other emergency. Of course you don't want to shut out all sun and air, but a metal bar or two will still admit plenty of both.

Incidentally, don't blame that security expert you had, or whom you may call at some future date, for including a seldom-used opening in his overall estimate (at some additional expense to you); he has no way of knowing the routine of occupants unless he is told. The following would be an extreme case, but possible just the same: You have no car, or if you do, you leave it always outside in driveway or street. The garage is used as a storage space only, nobody ever opens the large garage door, and furthermore nobody in the household has the strength to operate this heavy, outdated, rusty piece of machinery. Only that small side door is ever used. Why then waste the money on expensive electronic equipment to guard the main door, when a simple hasp or two, secured with padlocks, can seal this opening very effectively from the inside.

Right you are, "sealing" in our sense does not mean air-, water-, and windproof, it is merely the process of denying entrance from the outside, thus, in most cases, making operation from the inside more cumbersome than merely turning one knob.

The "Handle"

No matter how neglected that poor back door has been until now, there is an excellent chance that it has had right along one security device known to all of us: the knob you turn to get in and out. Basically this unit is nothing more than a spindle, extending through both sides of the door, which activates the latch to open the door.

This unit is important, even if it has no other locking mechanism whatsoever. Not only will it keep the dog out and the small baby in, but it will prevent the door from flying open in the breeze at a time when Adolf stands outside, looks, listens, then steps in. Let's face it, how many locks do people bother with during the routine activities of any day? At night, it's different, but in daylight hours a door gets slammed, and off we go. Since it is the only device that most people are willing to operate during the course of a busy day, let us go into some detail.

In its simplest form, there is no lock of any kind combined with this unit and within the house (bedroom to hall) it serves only to keep the door closed. As long as the spindle retracts the latch, we can be satisfied.

Next step up the ladder to added complications would be the door we want to lock from one side only, such as the one atop the basement stairs, leading into the rest of our living quarters, or the back door into the garage. Here we need no complicated keys, merely a built-in locking device that can normally be activated from a small extension on the spindle that extends through the doorknob, or a small lever extension on one side.

Unlike the first door, which has only to keep out flies, we expect this door to do more for us. In order to help it do a job, let us understand a bit about its insides. Somebody drilled a hole about two inches wide into the face of the door to accommodate a rather skinny spindle. Another one-inch hole was drilled at right angles to connect the larger hole to the outside world via a more or less sturdy latch. In effect, then, we have nothing more nor less than the age-old action of a simple sliding bolt which we pull back from its extended position so that we may open the door.

Although this basically simple system has long been effective, it is not exactly foolproof. Because spindle and latch are not welded, bolted, or glued together, it is a simple matter to extract the latch once the cylinder is pushed through its oversized hole. Why should Adolf want to start manipulating the mechanism when a simple one-two-three operation will remove the entire guts of the door? Let's understand why this has become a routine and commonplace operation.

To give us privacy in our bathroom, manufacturers incorporated one-way locks into the existing door latch. This simple addition caused havoc. Police had to break down doors to rescue little Johnny who had locked himself in, firemen had to enter bathroom windows to free a bather who had slipped in the tub, and doctors had to help hysterical relatives on the other side of the locked door live through this very traumatic experience.

Yankee ingenuity came up with many simple, effective solutions to this problem. Notice that small hole either in the center of the doorknob, or just below it in the escutcheon plate. Insertion of a nail or tiny screwdriver will unlock this door from the outside. If there is no hole, pushing the knob firmly and then turning it will open this door readily. No matter what make or type of construction your present lock might be, the chances are that it has this built-in "safety valve." Locks of this type do not carry a label "for bathroom use only" simply because they can be employed in various other places where privacy is desired. Therefore, *we must clearly distinguish between privacy and security, depending on what is required.*

A "safety valve" on an outside door would become an open invitation for Adolf—and we certainly don't want that. But there is an-other consideration. When used for privacy only, it makes little dif-ference whether this lock is mounted (spindle or cylinder) from the inside or outside. For security purposes, this factor is of great im-portance. By the same token—that somebody was able to complete the installation from the outside—Adolf and his more or less educated buddies can reverse this procedure.

Operation One Two Three

A door by itself is of no use whatsoever unless it is securely held in place. The strongest lock at one side of the door does no good if the hinges at the other end don't perform their function properly. And none of the hardware can be considered secure if there is a chance to remove it from the *outside*.

Door, doorknobs, latch, escutcheon plates, everything can look not only big, sturdy, and beautiful but also terribly secure. But wait, what are those two small screws doing on the escutcheon plate facing out? Simply this: They were the last pieces put in place when the entire locking mechanism was mounted. To remove them takes no more than an ordinary screwdriver. Removing them means the escutcheon plate and knob fall into your hand, which in turn exposes the spindle, and Adolf pushes the entire insides onto your kitchen floor. Of course, he is "in," since nothing holds the latch in place any longer.

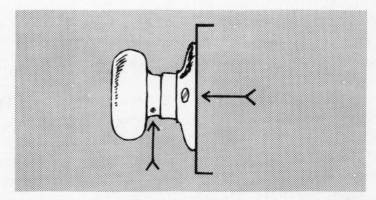

*Exposed screws in knob or escutcheon plate on outside of house
make lock worthless.*

Less effort is required for the door having a tiny hole under the outside knob instead of the two screws mentioned in the first operation. All that is required here is release of a catch, which then has the same effect as turning two screws in the earlier model. Even Adolf's kid sister is completely familiar with these simple operations.

To sum it all up, this simply is the wrong lock if we want to use it for security. A very similar type, which affords no access whatsoever into the inner workings from Adolf's side, is quite effective. Let's make sure you know which is in your door now.

Back Outside

One final look at our present lock. No hole, no screws—good. Escutcheon plate cannot be turned from the outside? All right then, let's leave it alone for awhile.

If by some method it is possible to get into the mechanism from the outside, then

1. Let us replace the lock or
2. Consider it only a means to keep out flies or
3. At least replace screws with type which can be turned only one way (clockwise).

This special type of screw finds extensive use in public places to prevent patrons from walking off with mirrors, cabinets, towel racks, and so forth. If not readily available, filing down the head of the existing screw will accomplish the same purpose. Neither method is a 100 percent sure cure for screw removal; they are, however, effective delaying devices. The same treatment should be given any other screw which holds hinge, peephole, or what have you, if it can be tampered with from the outside. But before replacing present screws, remember that removal will become a problem should you want to replace the present lock at some future date.

Latches and Bolts

The "business end" of any locking device is the part which in some way connects the door with the frame. If this piece of steel, known as latch or bolt, is pushed into the locking position only by a spring, as is the case with the lock above, it is reasonable to assume that anyone who can reach this important link in our security chain can overcome the negligible force of the spring by a slight counterpush, unless you are blessed with a latch guard (see Chapter 16). Tools for this operation need be no stronger or more complicated in design than the laminated identification or credit card you carry in your purse or wallet right now.

Yes, you have read about this easy way of gaining entry in local newspapers; you have been warned about it by your police department. Despite these warnings, can you honestly say that *every member* of the household takes the time actually to lock the door with the help of a key when leaving, especially on a shcrt errand? We all know we should, just as we should give up smoking too. But do we?

In order for us to be able to slam the door shut and be on our way, the latch must be beveled. To assist this very simple latch to do any kind of a security job, we must protect the beveled portion. A few inches of angle iron, a strip of metal in the right place, will protect this strategic area very nicely. When mounting this protection,

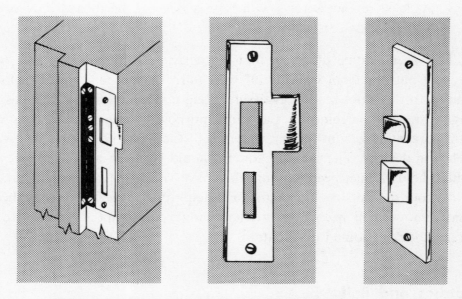

(Left) A strip of metal will protect against attack on that vulnerable bevelled latch. (Center) This innocent lock strike must be secure— lock and door depend on it. (Right) A vulnerable bevelled latch can be backed by a sturdy dead bolt.

you will keep in mind what we said about access to screws, won't you?

While in this area, a closer look at the lock strike would not hurt. Are the screws too small? Is the hole too big for the present screw? An ordinary toothpick, inserted in the hole, will give the screw better holding power if the hole is too large. While fiddling with this plate, you might also want to eliminate that draft because the door did not close tight enough all last winter. However, the important thing is that the latch engage firmly in the lock strike after completion of this operation.

This book cannot hope to cover every one of the thousands of effective locks already on the market. Besides, each will be glorified, praised, and explained in more detail by the manufacturer once you start shopping for an item that may suit you best. Very few sales pitches, geared to selling you better locks, will concern themselves with the present door or mounting. Further, after purchase of this lock, will every member make full use of it, or will we go right back to slamming the door?

No matter how complicated, secure, or expensive the new lock you have in mind may be, it will not be big enough to fill the opening now occupied by your door. What we mean, of course, is that it will only hold firmly *a door to a frame,* and this new lock will be dependent on both of these existing items to give you the security you want. The strongest catch at the end of Rover's leash will not keep him from running away if both collar and leash are ready to break at the slightest pull.

How Many Locks?

So far we have only looked at one lock, and a very simple one at that. No matter what the situation, or what the construction of your door may be, we strongly urge the installation of one other additional device, at least for night and vacation use. The reason we want to mention number before type of lock is simply that an overly cautious person might go shopping for any and all of the devices mentioned on the following pages and then, when fire or other emergency comes along, need umpteen minutes to get outside.

How many then? Sorry. Nobody in this world has the solution to that question. It will greatly depend on your own situation and need, but as a guide:

1. One lonely lock, no matter how good, is not considered sufficient.
2. Two or three locking devices sound reasonable for just about any situation.
3. More than three devices can very well make for a firetrap.

And for the purpose of this number game, we include everything from complicated machinery to the simple, yet effective, old-fashioned sliding bolt.

Finally: a Key

In common use, for front as well as back doors, is the above described lock with the addition of a keyhole on the outside. At the same moment you are happy that we finally got to something as sophisticated as a key, you also note that it is an item on which we have relied for generations, and which is merely another familiar piece of personal gear. You know that a key opens the door. You also know that you shouldn't lose it. And is that really all that counts? No, not for Adolf and his friends.

The bad boys would much rather circumvent any locking device than start tedious "picking." Arrest records show that they are staying away from the old art of picking more and more. However, if the picking is made so easy that it takes less time than it takes to get a screwdriver out of the rear pocket, Adolf will have a go at it. And go he will, since *any* lock that has an opening large enough to

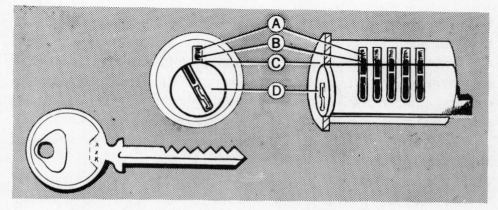

(Above) This makes your door lock tick: Springs (A) push drivers (B) across sheer line (C) preventing plug (D) from being turned without proper key. Front view shows lock partly opened while lengthwise cut shows locked position.

admit a key has an opening large enough to be picked.

Because we cannot change this fact, let us see what makes matters so easy at times for Adolf. The reason we need a key, to begin with, is that a number of pins, or wafers, or other little devils, have been placed in such a manner inside the lock that they extend from the stationary portion (cylinder) into the revolving part (plug), thus preventing any turning action. To be effective, they should be of various lengths, so that they line up properly only with the correct key.

With all this new-found wisdom, let's take a closer look at that familiar key in your pocket. Are hills and dales (cuts) in that key all of identical depth or so close to being identical that it is difficult to tell which one might be a bit deeper? If that indeed is so, we also know that all those little gadgets inside must be the same length. It follows then that a straight piece of just about anything in Adolf's pocket can open this door in the same time it takes the proper key to do it.

Throw away the lock? Not necessarily. Find a locksmith who will replace one or two of the pins with longer or shorter ones, then have him cut a new key, and you are as secure as the next fellow. Incidentally, you can have this very same operation performed when moving into a new home. Hint: Instead of buying new locks, invest in this simple operation of swapping number-two pin for number-four position. After all, it's these small gadgets inside your lock that determine who can get in and who can't, not the appearance of the shiny brass outside.

Properly made and properly installed, this lock offers a certain amount of protection. Since it becomes rather difficult in some cases to protect the beveled latch employed here, the addition of a "dead bolt" is highly recommended. Unlike the beveled variety, this fellow will not be budged by either identification card or much stronger tricky instruments. One drawback: This bolt has to be activated by a key to go into the locked position; its mere presence inside the door does absolutely no good. A dead bolt can either be incorporated into the existing door lock, or can stand all by itself on its own two feet, either above or below the doorknob. If operation can be effected only from the inside, it can serve as a most useful night latch; key operation from the outside gives this same bolt a 24-hour capability.

A Strange Arm

Before going into details on any additional locking devices, let us first see if one of your back doors (like so many) has a good-sized window built right into it. If not, consider yourself lucky, and skip the next few paragraphs. If the answer is "yes," please remember that you and I have known how to break plain window glass since we were big enough to heave a ball. Adolf's method of getting through glass is more sophisticated, but the end result is pretty much the same.

We can install a different door. Or we can put iron bars so close together that the windowpane is almost completely hidden. But one costs money, the other is not exactly free and will probably not look very pretty. The reason this window becomes desirable to Adolf is not because he can crawl through it (it is probably too small for that), but that this is the smallest windowpane with the biggest payoff. Large windows will break just about as easily, but did you ever listen to the terrific noise they make?

Here, then, is a small window—little noise, with an opening large enough for one arm to get through comfortably. Adolf is no dope. He knows that this arm will do him absolutely no good, unless it can reach and open the lock(s) that hold this door in place.

And on the other side of this door there is really not a thing to worry about (except a small broken window), as long as we can keep that door locked despite an arm, hand, and five fingers on *our* side. Impossible? Not at all. First of all, that door is approximately seven feet high. Even among real tall fellows you will have difficulty finding one with sufficient reach to get to the extreme top *and* bottom. Why not place a simple device at top and bottom? We have relied on keys to guard the outside of our door—why not install one of the many types of locks available which will operate from the *inside* as well as outside with a key? For an investment of approximately 25 cents, we can keep an extra key for emergency use near this door at all times—just outside the reach of any arm that might find its way through the glass.

Of course, a strange arm in your own kitchen is no pleasant experience, but unpleasant things can happen. The arm was not mentioned to worry you, but to let you know that proper precautions render it harmless. As we go back to our locking devices, let's keep the arm in mind when we start mounting additional locks.

Decisions, Decisions

The number of effective devices on the market today is fantastic. Here we will discuss only those which will actually keep your door locked; for alarm systems see Chapter 16.

A well-constructed, sturdy sliding or barrel bolt at the extreme top and bottom of the door can be quite effective, providing it cannot be reached through a crack between door and frame. Next in line for simplicity is the well-tested chain. We all know what it looks like, we all know how it operates, many of us use it properly when answering the door for a stranger, knowing that his foot is really all he can get in the door.

But how many know the ridiculously simple ways in which Adolf and his well-educated friends can nullify this pillar of our security?

No, we are not speaking of cutting or forcing anything in or near this security mechanism; neither do we have any type of special equipment in mind. Frightening is the fact that everyday household items are used to effect this simplest of operations in less than ten seconds—and if that were not enough, Adolf also has his choice of at least two equally efficient and equally easy methods.

Of the millions of chains in worldwide use, 99.9 percent were not mounted in their present position because that is where they are most effective, but because that is where Grandpa mounted his, that's where Pa mounted his along with all the neighbors, and that's "where a chain ought to be." If you now have a chain, and you are among the 99.9 percent mentioned earlier, your chain is mounted with chain portion and slide for chain knob at the same height, just about as

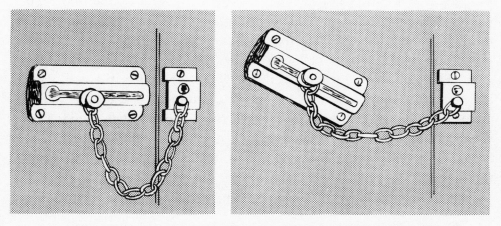

(Left) Is your chain mounted this close together? (Right) The same chain can offer real protection when mounted like this.

close together as possible. (Even the sturdiest of chains, by the way, will do little for the security of your home if the screws that fasten it are too small. Measure the thickness of your door, then buy well-made screws which are almost of the same dimension, and throw away the pretty, but short, screws that came with this chain.)

In order not to give "aid and comfort to the enemy" we are not about to divulge any methods by which this chain can be opened surreptitiously by unauthorized persons, but since for every measure there is a countermeasure, we will tell you how to counteract attempts at unauthorized entry.

1. Mount chain in such a way that it must be stretched *its full length* in order for knob at end of chain to reach into enlarged portion of slide.

2. Mount the slide just above, and at a slant toward the chain mounting.

When checking this new, unorthodox installation for security, please don't worry if you can still get a hand, or even an arm through the opening. To open any chain by reaching all the way around to unlock the chain from the slide takes an awfully long chain, and even your previous installation job was good enough to prevent such child's play. We are, of course, aware of many polished tricks of the trade, and through this new installation have foiled Adolf's advanced methods.

To check your new installation for beauty, don't ask friends or neighbors, they probably won't appreciate this very strange arrangement. If anyone objects too violently to drilling new holes for the chain slide, especially in the front door, don't make an issue of it. But please *twist* the chain before hooking it up to lock the door. This will at least shorten the chain somewhat and make entry not quite as easy. Incidentally, there is no law that says another chain can't be mounted (in the proper fashion) below the doorknob, or way down.

A rather effective lock is available which combines the chain with a key-operated lock. Among the many advantages is the fact that the chain can be locked in place from the outside when leaving the premises, and can remain in the locked position while nobody is at home. This very same chain can also be locked in place when the family is in the house, and an ordinary knob-slide action can be employed to leave in a hurry during an emergency. Because of this emergency feature, it is important that this chain be mounted in the same manner as the ordinary chain described earlier.

You Be the Judge

Just about the most effective type of lock you can get employs the vertical bolt, and is available in various and sundry editions. It is mounted on the inside of the door, away from most of the danger, and can be had with hardened steel bolts, the addition of a chain, and with or without key operation.

Now *you* are ready to check for yourself just what is needed in your situation. Do you have to guard especially against:

1. Shove (with card or knife)
2. Pick
3. Spread
4. Reach from inside

or possibly against all four?

Take another look at the last two types of lock. You no doubt will realize that they fill the bill for just about any situation.

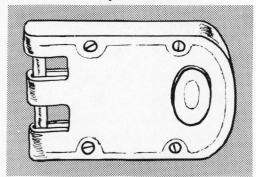

An effective vertical bolt.

Glass

Window glass is a wonderful invention, but *not from a security standpoint*. Before this invention, a hole in the wall was just that, and was treated as such. It was secured with shutters or boards against the enemy. Along came window glass to fill the hole, and we feel secure. Not so with our "old-fashioned" cousins, aunts, or parents in faraway countries. They secure their windows with steel bars, shutters, or some other sturdy material even today.

We are not about to suggest bars for all windows. Most of us are in agreement about leaving windows the way they now are, and if any changes are to be made, even more and bigger openings will be used.

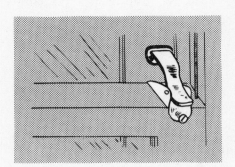 

(Left) Simple rubber-tipped lever secures double-hung window.
(Right) Expanding latch lock.

Already getting worried about all the glass in your home? Don't. Bringing "the great outdoors into your living room" with the use of larger sliding doors and picture windows is only part of the trend. Take a look at new office buildings, new store or bank fronts, or the new United States embassies and consulates throughout the world.

If none of these people are too worried about protecting merchandise, money, or state secrets despite this abundance of glass, then let us see what you can do to prevent illegal entry. In order to save time, shall we assume that you neither have bulletproof glass in all your windows now, nor are you willing to spend thousands to have it installed.

As with doors, on which we spent so much time, we must be selective about the type of device, the number of devices, and the actual need, depending on the location, size, and type of window. Adolf is not a noisy fellow; he most certainly is not foolish enough to break any good-sized window when he knows that this action on his part can bring speedy arrest.

But you read about the thieves who broke a large show window in downtown Manhattan, right on busy Fifth Avenue. Why was this done? Because the huge payoff was not only in full view, but also within easy reach. The entire operation took only seconds and a lot of guts, but it also had a guaranteed pot o' gold at its conclusion. The moral of this story is not to keep all your jewelry on display next to one of your windows, or our noise theory, at least part of it, will go right out that same window along with your beads. Let us keep in mind the big difference between *reaching* through a small hole to grab valuables and *removing* an entire window to attempt entry.

For various and sundry reasons, neither picture windows, box windows, nor any other permanently installed area of glass are likely to be selected as a point of entry. Only if you are the extremely cautious type, and only after all operable windows have been secured, would an alarm system be suggested for this type of opening. A metallic ribbon, which activates an alarm when the glass is broken, can be placed around the outer edges of these openings without spoiling their beauty. A small vibration sensor contact will be even less noticeable.

Break Glass?

Since we have become such experts by now about putting ourselves into Adolf's shoes, let's take a look at all windows collectively. Why break any pane at any time when in nine homes out of ten there is at least one window that either stands open, is closed but not locked, or has a broken or ineffective lock.

We are not about to repeat all the techniques that can be employed for opening doors (without breaking them), but let us keep these methods in mind when securing windows. Example: That traditional double-hung window in all probability has a traditional sash-locking device by which one half-moon-shaped piece of metal engages the other. If top and bottom portion are completely joined, this is not a bad locking device, but how often did you close one of these in a hurry, leaving the two pieces barely touching each other? Or how about that one lock where it has been impossible to get those two halves together properly ever since you moved into the house? Just as it is no great trick to insert something between door and jamb, it is even less difficult to reach from the outside between the top and bottom window frames and disengage an improperly locked gadget—and it's noiseless.

We know that Adolf will continue to look for the easiest and best method of entry. He knows that we have made life extremely easy for him through a certain amount of laxity and carelessness. Leaving a door open for him is only slightly worse than leaving an accessible window not properly secured.

More Windows

Many existing locks are sufficient to lock the window in a completely closed position, but since admittance of fresh air is one of the major reasons for having windows to begin with, let us see what can be done for that partially open window. For the previously mentioned double-hung window, an extremely simple lever-type gadget can be installed, which becomes tighter and more effective the harder a person attempts to open the partially open window. The trouble is, this particular unit can be used only with frames that slide up and down. Besides, it does not have a key-operated lock, and therefore it could be nullified by someone breaking part of the windowpane in order to reach inside.

Effective for almost any type of window are several kinds of key-operated locking bolts or expanding latch types of locks. Not only can they lock the window securely in place when closed, but even more important, in the partially open position. And for the purpose of security, let us treat that largest of all glass area, our sliding door, as just another oversized window.

As was the case with doors, when we locked them from the inside with the help of a key, here too it is strongly urged that the proper key be left close to the window for emergency use. Adolf gives breaking glass a second (respectful) thought before exposing himself to this danger; then why expose your own family to the hazard of having to break glass in case of fire. When we speak of having the key handy, we do not mean having all security keys in one safe place. We mean having each individual key within a few feet of corresponding lock, in a place well known to all occupants.

The ugly duckling, or neglected member of the window family, can normally be found in the basement. Not pretty, true, but terribly important to Adolf and his friends.

Note that every one of these openings is large enough to admit a full-grown man. Most of them are well hidden by foundation planting or other growth, giving a person on the outside a chance to inspect them more closely, undetected. Note also that of all the security hardware which was in the house when you moved in, this is the cheapest, least effective, mounted in the most hurried way. Not only that, but when winter comes and storm windows are added to all the other windows (making Adolf's entry more time-consuming and difficult), nobody bothers to include storms for the basement. Strange, but all too often true.

Not only can ordinary bricks *break* windows, but the author inspected one home in which bricks were actually used to *replace* each and every basement window. The owner had engaged a bricklayer to seal off all basement windows permanently. Now this drastic method is neither recommended nor is it necessary for protection.

Installing one or even two steel bars across that most vulnerable of windows is actually as complex a method as would be suggested here for the ordinary household.

A good point of debarkation for this particular phase of our security check would be a closer inspection of existing security devices, such as they are. Could it be that you have one of those two-cents-per-dozen butterflies on every window? The single screw that is supposed to hold this poor thing in place may be much too short to withstand even a slight push, or if long enough it may be awfully loose from use. Let's double-check it, just in case this is the window lucky enough to be selected by Adolf.

Since here so often neatness does not count quite as many points as in the rest of the house, you can really let your imagination run wild and come up with almost anything to secure these openings. Add inexpensive ordinary barrel bolts, or latches, or chains that are no longer pretty enough to stay mounted on the front door.

There might be a window or two which for some reason or other you cannot operate or do not need for ventilation. Mounting a separate windowpane on the outside permanently will not only give you protection against dust and dirt in summer, against cold in winter, but also year-round added protection against forced entry. Some ready-made basement storm windows come with a permanent screen mounted in a frame. The window can be removed for summer ventilation, but the screen remains as another delaying device between the outside and the existing window.

Just as an ordinary padlock sealed off that seldom-used garage door, another one, also mounted on the inside, can do an effective job here. A padlock would not look right? Then how about two sturdy screws, one through each of the corners opposite the hinges?

Hinges? Has anybody ever taken a look at those? As with a door, there is not much sense in securing one side of the frame when the other can easily be removed. The chances of finding only two screws where there should be six are much greater here than at the back door, especially if the hinges are on the outside, because to reach these hinges the workman who was supposed to put them in probably had to stoop down or kneel.

Curtains

No matter how tall or short the Adolf in your neighborhood is, he can look into each of the basement windows. There is probably not one individual who walks on your grounds who cannot effortlessly take inventory of all there is to see in your basement.

The normal reaction to this bit of information might be, "So what? If they want to come in to help me clean, let them." And you are so right, for there are probably no diamonds, furs, or any other valuables stored down there. Then what is the point?

That item in your basement which you consider of little or no value may be just the thing some young or not so young lad is looking for. When my family and I moved to new quarters in Europe, before there was a chance to secure everything, the basement was broken into. The only item stolen was a dilapidated air rifle that had been on top of the workbench waiting to be fixed; the workbench was directly under one of the windows. (The rifle was recovered from one of the neighborhood boys the same day.) But once inside, your intruder may just want to continue on a shopping trip through the rest of the house. Our uninvited European visitor was barred from the rest of the house by a truly sturdy old-fashioned locked door, but why invite him this far? This is where added security devices can be linked with camouflage.

Please do not feel smug about the security of your basement merely because it contains nothing of value, and leave off curtains to prove to the world that there really is nothing to take. The word "curtain" is used loosely here; any type of leftover material, held in place by thumbtacks if you like, will do a satisfactory job of not leading the innocent into temptation, or giving the hardened criminal advance information about where he might stumble over something, causing noise.

After securing all basement windows, we might give more than a casual glance at the door between the basement and the rest of the house. Not that we expect anybody to sneak into our basement after we have secured it, but when all alone at night we might like to know that a sturdy door with properly placed locks is between us and the strange noise we heard, or thought we heard, emanating from the basement.

-4-

Inside Your Apartment

It is much easier to protect an apartment than it is to protect any one-family house.

The chances are good that you do not have too many back doors, too many basement windows, and that most of your regular windows (no matter what type) are difficult to reach from the outside. But don't let these circumstances by themselves lull you into a feeling of security. We do not want to be misunderstood here, because all it takes for Adolf to make his entrance is *one* unreliable door or window.

No doubt that apartment door is not much different from doors described previously. What we suggest is that you make use of those features described earlier which are best suited for your particular needs.

In most cases a homeowner can observe the person at the front or back door from some nearby window, without opening the door to a stranger. Since this is impossible in most apartment houses, the installation of a peephole, also known as an "interviewer" or "spy," is suggested. Before investing, though, check that it does not have only window glass for lenses, since that will give rather limited vision. Wide-angle lenses are available at nominal cost. Some come complete with nameplate holder.

A word of caution before you slide name into holder, if you are one of those women who live alone, do not advertise this fact to Adolf and his friends. Neither Miss Kaufmann nor Karen Kaufmann leaves much doubt in anyone's mind about the occupant. Use K. Kaufmann instead, and keep 'em guessing.

Who Is It?

How often in our lives have we asked: "Who is it?" We asked in good faith, and for some strange reason most of us never bothered to doubt that the reply was given in the same good faith. Well, times seem to change, and some people are getting more security-conscious. With the help of the widely used peephole we can recognize all our friends, neighbors, and other welcome guests. But what about the other persons who come to that very same door, the ones we have never seen before?

You may decide not to open the door to any stranger, may even be able to keep this rule for an entire week or two. But then there is the fellow who comes with a telegram marked "urgent," or the one who needs your signature before he can leave a very interesting, expensively wrapped package or bouquet of flowers. How long will you be able to abide by your own rules?

Finally you give in to temptation, open the door because "he looked all right." *How can anyone tell what goes on in another person's mind simply by looking at him?*

To give a signature or to receive a package, the homeowner can open one of his windows a bit, whereas the apartment dweller is normally not that fortunate. For that reason we must provide this door with some sturdy gadget which will allow us to open it slightly without admitting an unwanted stranger. For that purpose the old reliable chain is still the most effective device available.

The Fire Escape

Movies, TV, and many storytellers have glamorized a creature known as the "cat burglar." He is not fictional, he does exist, but so does the American bald eagle. Both have become rather rare birds. This fact should not make us disregard them, but on the other hand not let us lose sleep waiting for a visit from either one.

Why do we pass over this cat-burglar profession so blithely? Because the installation of outside fire escapes has been one of the greatest boons to the burglary industry. "Why risk my neck when perfectly good stairs are provided?" says Adolf to himself, and he is so right. The legislator, the builder, and the fire chief had a perfectly good reason to put a contraption like this where they put it. We fear fires, and respect the men who fight them.

But, fire escapes are fringe benefits for every bad guy who is able to negotiate a staircase. That this "stairway to a fortune" does not normally start at street level keeps stray elephants from bending the bottom steps. But what about the top of this steel extravaganza? Of course the top is neither secured nor locked in any way—that would be contrary to just about every fire regulation.

Although Adolf and his clan may not abide by every law and regulation, they do know about their existence and take advantage of those which will benefit them. They know about the "open door policy" as it pertains to fire escapes, and they know enough to find the "up" button on the elevator. After all, that is all it takes, a ride to the top floor, and a few steps to the roof. Everybody knows that no respectable stray elephant walks on rooftops, therefore no special precautions of any type have been taken here.

Regulations permitting, and landlord willing, the doors leading to the roof could be treated, latched, and secured by methods similar to those recommended for front doors of apartment buildings, with special fire escape provisions. But this in itself could lead to the very same problems that we encountered at the front door earlier, only here the traffic would be lovers, sunbathers, or stargazers.

Even if all the problems in *your own* apartment house can be solved, how about security at the adjoining building? Not to frighten you, but how about the fellow who used a pass key to break into the apartment above or below yours? At this moment he may be shopping for additional loot via the same fire escape. How reassuring for Adolf that none of these windows has been closed permanently, since all must remain what they were meant to be, escapes.

Post a twenty-four-hour guard here? An excellent idea, but a bit costly in the long run. Seriously, we feel so strongly about this one security hazard that we urge you to take full advantage of every device and alarm that will make entry as difficult as possible and yet allow this same window to be used as an escape in case of emergency.

Securing the opening under discussion here is not easy. It could be closed completely with something like a hinged folding steel gate secured from the inside with a padlock. But even if this method is legal in your area, would you *want* to use it? The truly difficult question to answer is how far do we want to go with all this, yet not bar the way for that most welcome fireman who may attempt to enter through this very same opening on his mission of mercy. We can open the gate for him—providing we are not trapped by flames or overcome by fumes.

As a guideline then: Use any and all hardware needed to force an intruder to break glass, with the alarm system best suited to your situation. In case of emergency you will be able to get *out*, firemen will be able to get *in*, and neither of you will worry about alarms at a time like that.

-5-

Burglars and Burglaries

What was covered in the previous chapters is known as a "security survey" by security officers throughout the world. They follow the same type of pattern we used, but they do it to secure a large industrial plant or a faraway embassy. To do a single job properly will take from several weeks to a few months, depending on the size of the installation and the manpower available. Nobody can expect you to complete a survey of your own living quarters overnight. Nobody does. But until that great day comes when all your security measures are in place, here are a few hints that may prove helpful.

Should you become aware of a burglar inside your home while you are near an exit door, leave the house quickly and summon the police from your neighbor's house. In case you can't leave undetected, lock all the doors between yourself and the intruder, then phone the police or try to summon help by shouting through an open window. True, dialing "O" for operator will eventually get you in touch with the police, but you can save precious seconds by keeping emergency numbers pasted right on or near your phone. You can possibly hasten the arrival of help even more by finding out *now* whether the number to call is police headquarters, with its busy communication system, or the local precinct house.

Confrontation with the intruder should be avoided if at all possible, but in case it can't, you will benefit from reading Chapter 15 (self-defense).

If you discover, upon return to home or apartment, that you have been burglarized, don't touch or move anything—and see to it that others don't either. Before calling the police, try to determine quickly that it *was* a burglary and not a fight between your daughter and prospective son-in-law that caused the commotion in your living room. Be as helpful and honest with investigating detectives as possible. Don't make positive statements about your having locked the back door before leaving, *unless you are sure*. "Positive" statements, which later prove wrong, make the investigation much more difficult than no statement at all. Point out any item which is not your property—it may have been left by the burglar.

Don't bother to inquire about the approximate time you may expect the return of your stolen valuables. Police will try, but the chances of recovery of stolen property are minute. You yourself can assist greatly, before anything is stolen, by preparing an inventory of valuables. If possible, list the date and place of purchase, cost, description, serial number, and any special markings of your most valuable possessions. Photographs of jewelry or antiques can be of great assistance in future identification and possible recovery. Remember that collections of both stolen and "abandoned" goods, for which the rightful owner cannot be located, are kept only a limited time, and then disposed of at public auction.

Problems?

Can't find the serial number on your son's bike? If it is not six inches under the seat on the frame, look on either side of the frame under the sprocket. Your wife never took the time to have her initials embroidered inside her full-length mink coat, and now it looks pretty much like all the others up and down the street? Then (while she is not looking) take some India or laundry ink and put her initials, or some other identifying mark, a few inches up inside the lining of one sleeve.

Any other similar problems?

Contact your insurance agent or the police. Both will be more than glad to give you advice, since you will be making their job easier in case something happens to your property. Many insurance companies will be happy to furnish you with "inventory sheets" which are yours for the asking.

Conducting a security survey and completing an inventory sheet are time-consuming chores. You have only limited time to spare, and are probably not overjoyed at the prospect of "wasting" any of it on this type of activity. But before disregarding either of these assignments, consider the following:

1. Your family's and your own safety.
2. Stolen goods are hardly ever recovered.
3. Certain items are irreplaceable.
4. Insurance rates will go up in a burglarized home.
5. Insurance rates will start at a higher rate if you plan to change companies, since the application form for home insurance asks, "Have you ever submitted a claim for burglary?"
6. The traumatic experience of having been bound and gagged by

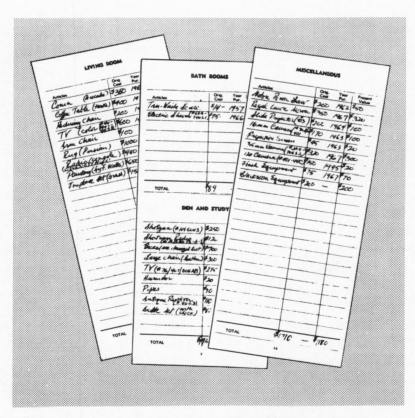

Inventory sheets such as these will enable you to prepare your loss claim accurately.

an intruder will live with you and your children for years to come—day and night.

Security surveys are normally followed by "security checks," which are conducted periodically to determine that all new items are in their proper location and working satisfactorily. It would be wise for you, at least once in a while, to inspect wires, switches, bulbs, bells, locks, or other items that have been installed to protect your home.

-6-

Visitor Control

The word "visitor" is used here in its broadest sense, but does not include any person or persons who will seek admittance by force or violence. We are no longer concerned with Adolf and his burglar tools, but plan to focus our attention on his cousin Benito. This fellow, too, is an expert in his field, who can appear at your front door in any number of disguises. Since Benito is not the only one who seeks admittance, and since we can't tell the players from the spectators without a program, we will cover all those who may at one time or other appear at your door.

But, with a strict policy of not opening the door to *any* stranger, it is logical to assume that Benito does not have a chance to penetrate that fortress of yours. We worked so hard at keeping Adolf out, why take a chance opening the door for his cousin?

We all know that anybody, even though he may have lives, secrets, or property to protect, at one time or other must admit strangers into his four walls. For the purpose of this chapter,

1. "Anybody" can be a government, a corporation, or a playboy in his pad.
2. "Stranger" can be anyone from a foreign diplomat to a meter

reader or newspaper boy.

3. "Four walls" could be a country, a sensitive installation, or a basement.

The biggest anybody, a government, will, like you, have visitors come to the door—foreign dignitaries arriving at the airport. Now, can you imagine a charming lady at Kennedy International Airport identifying herself as the Queen of Sheba? It would be terribly embarrassing to request identification from Her Majesty—but no government in its right mind would give royal treatment to anyone based on faked jewels and forged documents. Among civilized nations, one government announces to the other plans for the impending visit, and further correspondence arranges details.

Benito may arrive for his state visit at your door, dressed immaculately, with the unmistakable air of distinction about him, representing the bank that holds your mortgage or the corporation that owns the apartment house. He must check on the condition of the inside, he must do it now, and furthermore this inspection is terribly important for your own future. Certainly, he has papers to prove all this. Our question: What makes this bum, dressed in sheep's clothes, so different from Queeny? If indeed an inspection was necessary, his office should have sent word. Since they didn't, make him wait until you have had a chance to call his office.

Next in size would be a corporation. Even the biggest of these industrial giants must have social and business intercourse with the rest of the world. Keep all gates locked? Impossible. Hence, it may maintain a special department known as the Security Division, which in most cases is also responsible for this important function called visitor control.

Visitor control, of course, does not keep the repairman from getting to broken equipment in the plant, or the supplies from reaching their destination, but rather checks on identity, logs the visitor in and out, notifies personnel inside plant of the visitor's arrival, and depending on number of persons available for this service, escorts the visitor to his destination.

Again Benito stands outside your door, this time in coveralls, and with tools in his hand. He has played this game for quite some time, so that he not only talks convincingly, but even stole a union button for his cap to assure you that he is legit. He has to adjust all gas valves on the block, or check fuses in the entire apartment house, and is in a great hurry to finish the job. You have no visitor control bureau in your home to check him out, nor do we suggest you get one. What we do suggest is that you take a lesson from the fellows whose job it is to keep undesirables out. Inspect credentials closely, if you are familiar with the real document this particular company issues, or make a phone call to the organization he allegedly represents. He may get impatient, he may get mad, but both Benito as well as his legitimate counterpart know that a well-guarded company of any size would not admit him on his friendly smile alone. Why then should your home be any different?

The last, but by no means least, anybody is that happy-go-lucky playboy in his small, but plush, pad. If this individual householder does his own shopping, that eliminates admitting even delivery boys. Yet we could think of one hundred and one individuals who at times could have some business to take care of inside this inner sanctum, and would be welcome, too. Plumbing on the blink, rug needs shampooing, windows need cleaning, reception on color TV has to be tuned on location? Benito can think of many other excuses to come calling.

Somewhere in between the biggest and the smallest of these examples stands your front door, and your problems are really no different from those encountered above. Your door will swing open at some future date to admit someone you really don't know. Without proper precautions, this person may be Benito.

Looks Are Deceiving

Too many people actually believe they can tell a thief, a spy, or a user of narcotics simply by looking into his face. But ask a person trained along spy-catching lines, and he will tell you that it is as "easy" to point out a spy as it is to pick out a person who has had his tonsils removed. As a matter of fact, it is much easier to determine that tonsillectomy: Call a doctor and have the suspect open his mouth! A spy? Call a trained interrogator: After an hour, a day, or a week he may come up with some verdict, the length of time depending upon his training and the skill of the suspect. One thing is clear: *At this time it is impossible to distinguish a criminal from a noncriminal by visual inspection.*

Note that we said "visual inspection," which is a long way from observation over an extended period of time. We were speaking of looking at someone through the peephole of your apartment door, or opening that door as far as the chain will reach.

One of the most celebrated federal intelligence agents in the world once said that a phenomenal memory is the first prerequisite for becoming an effective intelligence agent. A solid memory can help you too—more than your presumed ability to tell a man's character and intentions by his looks. You will be a few steps ahead of Benito if you look from time to time at the posters in your local post office, or the pictures in your local newspaper depicting known hoodlums or criminals. A crook, like most of us, is a creature of habit; he may wear his hat in the same way, cut his hair at a conspicuous length, or have any one of a thousand little idiosyncracies in his behavior.

It is also helpful to get to know what a bona fide police badge looks like, to remember what kind of identification a *real* telephone repairman carries, and so forth.

Staying alert, reading descriptions of operators in your area in local newspapers, or checking with police on the most notorious crooks in your town will help identify certain *individuals*—though these precautions alone will not enable anyone to determine the bad from the good.

Remember: If you have any doubt, keep that door locked until you have *positive* identification!

Credentials

Regardless of how big the estate or the apartment house, the front door determines whether a caller gets in or stays out. We have said that looking at the "visitor" will not tell us who he really is. Asking for credentials *might* help. Credentials? We all know what credentials are—or should know.

We know that a good and well planned set of credentials should:

1. Give individual's name.
2. Show clear picture.

3. Give physical dimensions.
4. List physical characteristics.
5. Have signature of individual.
6. Have serial number of document.
7. Show name and address of company.

There are dozens of additional desirable items, such as fingerprints, telephone number of company, name of issuing official, expiration date of document, company or agency seal, etc. Hardly any two are alike, and leaving off or adding on additional lines in no way makes one method right and the other wrong.

Since there is no person on earth who can retain a mental picture of every set of credentials issued by all our government agencies, federal and local; by utility companies, and by the many private enterprises, to distinguish fake from real is no easy task. However: *You and you alone are the person in charge here. Let the caller feel that you have this situation well under control, and that you are not about to surrender your power over the yea or nay to anyone.*

"May I see your credentials" in most cases results in the caller pulling something halfway out of his pocket, and, if really cooperative, may even hold this something into the air. No more! Instead, say, "May I *have* your credentials," and expect to have this document delivered under or over the chain which still denies entry. This request alone may separate the real from the phony. Every person authorized to carry the credentials with which he is about to impress you will have no objection to handing them over for inspection. He may not like it, but he will comply with your request.

To give all of the clever answers you may expect from Benito right at this point would fill a good-sized volume. "Not allowed," "Against company policy," "They will come apart," "What's the matter, you blind or something?" are among the more common excuses.

Humbug, we say to that. The author carried a type of credential which had to be protected at all cost for twenty-four hours around the clock. Loss would have meant curtains. Yet, there was no objection to having an individual concerned about their authenticity inspect them closely.

And now that we hold something fairly official-looking in our hand, what do we look for? To look at the picture and to look at him might be a fine start. Ridiculous, you say, nobody is so clumsy that he attempts a foolish thing like stealing identification with someone else's picture. Then listen to this: During World War II security was being tested at a sensitive installation. An agent affixed Joseph Stalin's picture to a pass issued by that particular agency, and was able to enter, as well as leave, without being questioned. No, the agent did not look like Joe.

Fantastic—but allegedly true!

We can check whether a picture looks as though it is truly part of the original document, rather than one which replaced the picture of its true owner. Do print, paper, and lamination give the appearance of a homemade job? Has document expired? What about the back? Don't be surprised to discover that the back half has been peeled off completely, since Benito would not want you to see the height of original owner given as 4' 11" when his 6' 2" frame leans against your door at this very moment.

A bit of discretion and personal judgment on your part can, of course, go a long way in these proceedings. You expect a man from the phone company this afternoon. You inspect his credentials, have an idea what they should look like, inspect them, and find them in good order. No reason to give the fellow a hard time, or delay him unnecessarily.

Check 'em Out

A slight doubt in your mind remains about the authenticity of the caller? Don't you fret. By actual count we happen to have a million and one various ways of checking on him. Some of these methods may take a minute or even two, but then you have not forgotten about *you* being the only one in charge here, right? From the position in the driver's seat only you can determine what further action should be taken.

A person using stolen credentials will often have brains enough to memorize certain information given on these credentials, such as the name, at least. But while still holding credentials in your hand, how about asking about birthday, serial number of document, and such. Even Benito with all his cunning sometimes can be caught by one of these simple questions. And if he did take the trouble to memorize all the information given, it does appear strange when it takes an adult several seconds to give his birth date.

You don't have to be a handwriting expert to check a signature. True, it may not be foolproof to ask the stranger to sign his name in your presence, so that you may compare the signature on his identification with what he just wrote. But then, *so few people misspell their own name,* and again you will be amazed how easily a discrepancy can be detected. No paper and pencil handy? Then ask him to spell his full name, while you compare it with the way it was given on the credentials.

We are not going to fall for the old line about the girl in the office making a typographical error while preparing these credentials. If indeed this document was issued to "give title to credit and confidence," then it had better be letter perfect before we can be expected to respect it.

Not Convincing Enough

For some reason you are still not convinced. How about changing the conversation to other items. "May I have your driver's license?" might be a good start. If this stranger is really who he claims he is, he might get a bit impatient, but why should he refuse to give you his license? The name on the license will be identical with that on his credentials, as will be the rest of his personal statistics, and a signature for comparison. Don't overplay your part by asking him to recite the number on his driver's license. Some people don't even recall their automobile license number, let alone that mile-long figure on the operator's license.

In case cousin Benito did survive your scrutiny up to this point, he is getting terribly nervous by now. Being the cool customer he is, this nervousness might not show too badly on the outside, but on the inside only he knows how badly things really are going for him. Now this request for additional identification. There are enough fine upstanding citizens in this country who for some good reason do not have a driver's license. Yes, he could say that he does not own one, but what are the chances of his being what he claims to be (telephone representative, delivery man, salesman, or what have you) without also being a driver?

Although it sounds suspicious that he does not have an operator's license, it could just possibly be true. All right then, how about producing any other type of identification. Even if he claims to have lost all of his credit cards and burned his draft card, there should be a membership card to some organization, club, or group. In case he produces nothing, he has neither helped to instill greater confidence nor succeeded in exhausting the numerous ways of checking on him.

Make a Call

A call to the office or agency this fellow allegedly represents should of course help to shed light on his true identity. No, thank you, we don't want to hear the number from him, just name and address—we will look up the number ourselves in the book. Dialing the number he gives could, of course, connect us with his girl friend, who will swear to every lie he cares to tell us.

And once we are suspicious enough to make a call, we will make certain that there will be a completed, satisfactory call. Here again the honest fellow will be most anxious for us to get this call through as quickly as possible, while Benito comes up with some more or less plausible excuses why his office can't be reached. "There is never anybody in on Tuesday afternoons. Don't bother trying," "They are all out for coffee now anyway," or "We have a new girl at the switchboard, she wouldn't know me," "I just started working there, they won't recognize my name."

The string of well-rehearsed excuses Benito is able to offer is endless. Among the more sophisticated ones would be that he represents an extremely hush-hush government agency, and must talk to you in private on a confidential matter. The reason you cannot find his office listed in the telephone book, he claims, is because this supersecret organization is not listed. Bunk!

Just about all agencies have at least one telephone number listed in your local directory, possibly not location of office, but the telephone number is there for verification of a caller's story. "My office is not allowed to give you information about my identity" is also a mighty weak excuse, since the agency is of course anxious to have its cases completed as soon as possible, and therefore is more than willing to state that yes, indeed, your caller works for them.

"Just flew in from Washington this morning, nobody in this area knows me" may be another way to discourage calls for verification of identity. While you stand in the doorway, listening to this farfetched story, you feel that this caller could have come up with a more plausible tale to invade your home. His "story" might be the truth, but truth or not, we have made up our minds earlier that *once we are suspicious enough to make a call, we will make certain that there will be a completed, satisfactory call.* This fellow, no matter who he is, will not be any exception. This sounds harsh; it may even sound as though we are undermining trust and confidence in the efficiency of our own government. Not at all.

Government agents or officials are not the only ones who from time to time may have to operate away from their own home base. Detectives, insurance adjusters, and many others fall into this category. If any of them expect to be admitted by you, they had better stop at their own local agency, precinct, or branch office, and identify themselves first, and only then start ringing your doorbell. The fellow from that supersecret agency had better identify himself properly at a nearby organization listed under United States Government Agencies in the telephone directory, inform them that he will be working in this area for a certain length of time, and then try your doorbell. This simple but often neglected process is known as coordination. And why can we be so strict about demanding proof of identity, without making any exceptions? Because the legitimate caller at the door knows that *the burden of proving identity lies upon him who alleges it.*

Benito is probably aware of this too. He may have spent an extra few dollars to have some forger make a "perfect" document. He proudly presents this document as "proof positive" of his identity, hoping that you will honor it blindly. Something makes you suspicious, and this piece of paper becomes but one piece of evidence which, by itself, does not amount to proof. Hence the telephone call.

Wrong Address?

All this while you may well have been saying to yourself that no hot-shot, high-calibre investigator will ever come to *your* door. No need. Never had as much as a traffic ticket, and as for the spy angle, never even heard of a fellow named James Bond. Even so, there may be a perfectly legitimate person coming to that door of yours to ask a few questions. The reason for the visit could be that little Gregory from down the block is now sufficiently grown to be considered for a position of trust and confidence with the government, and he needs a security clearance for that. Or if a friend of yours applied for a pistol permit, you as character reference may have to be interviewed.

As you can see, there is an excellent chance that none of these interviews will hurt you, yet not to cooperate with those who request these interviews may mean that Gregory will have a tough time getting his position, and your friend may never get his permit.

Neither one of these examples would warrant a member from any "flying squad" to visit from far away, but the man about to leave as our Ambassador to lower Slobovia may have been your next door neighbor just recently. Somebody in Washington wants a few answers about him in a hurry—and there is your caller at the door. Not so farfetched, is it?

-7-

Informers

Up to this point, visitor control consisted only of screening the good from the bad, of weeding out Benito from legitimate callers. But there are other callers, legitimate callers, whom we must also consider. There is no reason, of course, to ask John, who has delivered milk faithfully for the past ten years, for identification. But think of all the others who sometimes enter your home. There are, for example: salesmen, routemen, repairmen, meter readers, census takers, mailmen, newsboys, bill collectors (looking for someone else), and all delivery fellows. These, in the performance of their duties, have a perfectly valid reason for being on your property, at your door, and even in your home. *But:* There might be just one who would possibly be tempted to steal if the worthwhile loot is displayed within easy reach at each of his visits.

We know people who consistently pay their paper boy his few pennies weekly out of that fancy cookie jar located in the kitchen. Nothing wrong with that, except that this young fellow has to watch the lady of the house remove ten- and twenty-dollar bills to get to the change at the bottom—if this jar is also the repository for Dad's pay. Is there any need to put this much temptation before a young man fifty-two times a year?

Though your milkman is more mature, there is no need leading him constantly into temptation either. When he delivers the milk and helpfully places it in your refrigerator, why prominently display all the jewelry you wore to last night's party?

How all these visitors can live through the dozens of temptations placed directly in front of them day after day is remarkable. For remaining honest citizens, most of them deserve much credit. In all these years the paper boy never reached into your cookie jar, although he was frequently left alone in that kitchen while he was getting a drink; and the milkman never took a single one of those glittering diamonds. But that is only part of the problem. Both the paper boy and milkman have friends—some of whom are not honest.

Have Friends, Will Talk

The danger of these visits does not lie in the dishonesty of one visitor so much as in his powers of observation. He may not be a trained spy, deliberately snooping around your home—but he is not an idiot, and does have a pair of eyes in his head. He also has friends, some of whom, perhaps without his knowledge, may collect cookies or diamonds—*if the collecting is made easy enough or attractive enough for them.*

We might call any of our visitors "unwitting sources" of valuable information, or "innocent informers" for one of their friends—one of whom could be using a substance called narcotics.

Nobody really knows how many users of narcotics there are in the world. Official guesstimates claim that 3 million people are "hopelessly addicted" in our country alone. Crime statistics show that during the most recent year for which figures are available, 37,802 were arrested in the United States. The fact that the *percentage increase* over the previous year was 31.3 for males and 32 for females is not half as startling as the following: *Arrests in connection with illegal use or sale of narcotics increased in a single year 40.4 percent for females under eighteen years of age and an almost unbelievable 74.4 percent for their male counterparts.* And you may safely bet your bottom dollar that not all the narcotics needed to satisfy these habits were paid for with certified cashier's checks. Most of the supply was purchased (and will continue to be purchased) by delivering stolen goods to the nearest fence, who cashes them for a fraction of their true value.

All this loot comes from somewhere. Information leading to loot could be innocently passed out by any of the above-named honest individuals. All it takes to become an "informer" is to mention stuffed cooky jars or jewels on the dresser; the owner of big ears will take it from there.

Before going any further, let us make clear that the occupations mentioned were picked only as examples, and that this incomplete list should in no way be construed as an imputation of guilt. Further, it would be completely unfair to accuse all narcotics users of being thieves, or to imply that this is the only group that produces dishonest persons.

Control

Of course, you cannot be expected to lock everything that is not glued down in your home into one burglarproof safe before answering the doorbell. If that big corporation locked up all valuable tools and stopped production every time they had a visitor, stockholders would soon cash in their chips. Then why not learn from them a bit, since theirs sounds like such an impossible task compared to the relatively small area we want to guard?

First, let us consider if it would not be more efficient and safer to pay the bill or sign that receipt at the door, rather than have the visitor escort us right to the hiding place of all our money.

It's not practical to carry a gas meter up to the door so that it can be read there by the meter reader. Well, we could make use of "modern science and delicate machinery" instead: Remember when Grandma had ice delivered for her icebox, and instead of making one trip to find out how much ice Grandma needed and another to deliver that amount, this brilliant iceman put a hunk of cardboard in Grandma's window, and with an indicator similar to the hand on a watch, the desired amount could be shown. This fancy "invention" can be used on every third, or tenth of the month, whenever the meter reader is expected. It can even today show him how much gas was used during the month, and eliminates the bother of opening the door for him.

Without working too hard at it, you can no doubt come up with many other ways of stopping the numerous, regular walks through the house by outsiders. If the trip is unavoidable and the stay will be short, there is no reason why you cannot furnish escort service. This will only take a few minutes of your time, and does not in any way have to be embarrassing. "I don't trust you" is not exactly the wording he would appreciate, but there is nothing wrong with showing the way, saying, "Let me get the lights for you," or "I'll get the kids' toys out of the way."

If the visit will be of longer duration, such as from a repairman, and no member of the household has the time to look over the fellow's shoulder while he does his work, it would be wise to remove valuables at least from plain sight. If it was not done beforehand, no honest workman will object to waiting for a second while you "clean up the mess" around his work area before he enters.

Don't like to be alone with any of them? Have him come after four when Dad is home, or on Saturday. Can't wait that long? Then inform him by phone that you will be home only between three and four in the afternoon. As soon as he agrees to come, invite one of your friendly neighbors to share a cup of coffee with you at that hour.

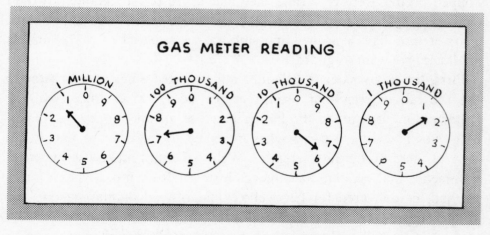

Placed in a window, this card can eliminate a stranger's walk through your house.

-8-

Servants, Aunts, and Children

So far we have dealt with two groups of people: Benito and his friends who will not be admitted, and those honest folk who will stay within our walls for a relatively short period of time. Now we'll add a third group, those who actually, or for all intents and purposes, are members of the immediate family.

To have warned you about possible dangers within these first two groups may have been tolerable, but to utter anything derogatory or unfavorable about this last selection is looking for trouble. The maid? Why, faithful Brenda has been with you for years, she's as honest as the day is long, and never harmed a fly. Besides, you did not just accept all those raving references when she first started to work for you without at least checking by phone with one or two prior employers.

Relatives? Certainly that sweet old aunt can be trusted. She has not only given each of the children a savings bond every birthday, she included you and the children in her will. To run a background check on her prior to her two-week stay with you would be preposterous.

Your own child? Of course he can be trusted. Then why bother to discuss this group at all?

Small Items of Value

Because no matter how careful we want to be, no matter how many warnings we heed from police and other sources, there will still be items of value in the home which for one reason or another can't remain in our safe deposit box until the moment we need them.

We are not speaking of large items now; we are concerned here with cash, which normally can't be insured; also with jewelry, valuable stamp or coin collections, and the like.

Whether the "small" amount of cash on hand is considered a fortune by someone else is immaterial to this discussion; the fact is that you will need at least *some* greenbacks handy. Jewelry was not bought to hibernate in a bank vault forever, and a true collector finds little satisfaction in viewing his collection only during visiting hours.

No matter how much of your property is safely stored (and rightly so) at some local institution with proper facilities, there will still be a portion remaining in the home.

Regarding this remaining portion, please don't say that in your particular case it is really nothing to worry about since there is so little value to it. Everything in life is relative. The man who wants to steal his way to financial independence and a life of luxury in South America may consider $100 peanuts, while the man desperate for just one more drink will consider his burglary, netting one dollar bill, a successful operation.

Secret (or Is It?)

To leave these valuables out in the open is foolish. For that reason you have already been in the habit of putting them in a more or less secure place, even found a good hiding place for the most valuable ones. You may have a small, fireproof strongbox or even a safe.

None of these items was put away because you were particularly worried about servant, aunt, or child taking them to the local market to swap them for dope or booze. You put them away to protect them. Much of the protection would be destroyed were the mere location known to an intruder. Since none of these items either belongs to or concerns the above three individuals, we feel there is no reason to reveal the location of their hiding place. If you have a large safe which, because of size, cannot be hidden, then it most certainly is not necessary to make everyone aware of its combination or the location of keys.

We stubbornly maintain that withholding information about the mere existence of these hiding places is the most effective aspect of protecting valuables. The less talk, the more protection. Too many people seem to agree with our own grandmother, who observed: *What good is knowing the biggest secret if you can't talk about it?*

-9-

Away from Home

You are planning a vacation. Wonderful! You already have made a list of all the things to be done before leaving: stop milk delivery, notify the post office to hold all your mail until your return, have a neighbor collect newspapers, fliers, and similar matter from your doorstep, and keep an eye on your place. Good!

It is only normal that you are excited, that you want to brag at least a little to anybody who is willing to listen. But do not "advertise" this pending absence to everyone. Remember that Adolf and his friends are seeking just such information. Why play into their hands?

If you are prominent enough to rate a write-up in the local paper about your vacation, try to have it printed *after* your return, not before. If the family car will be used for the trip, there is no need to leave it sitting in front of the house for hours with trunk and doors wide open, while a lengthy loading takes place.

Yet keeping the trip a complete secret from everyone is not wise. A good idea would be to leave your itinerary with a friend or neighbor, so you can be reached in an emergency. Leaving the description of your automobile, including the license number, may assist in locating you.

Furnishing your local police with a "Vacant Premises Report" will, in most locations, get you free periodic inspection by that friendly officer on the corner or by a cruising squad car. This protection applies to mansion as well as pad. But of course if several of your friends have keys, this vacant premise report could lead to embarrassing situations.

It goes without saying that you will do nothing to change the outward appearance of your place while you are gone, that is, if shades are not normally drawn fully all day, you will not leave them closed. You might ask a neighbor, or use one of the many new gadgets, to turn your lights on for some time each evening. For a few dollars, a friendly neighborhood kid will shovel snow or cut grass so that the grounds and home will not look deserted.

And please don't change the interior of your home too much during this period. We had occasion to look into the ground-floor living room of a vacationing family where every piece of furniture had been carefully covered with a large throw cloth, giving it a museum-like appearance.

Have a lovely vacation, return safely, and *then* tell all about it, not before.

Not Far from Home

Perhaps you have been doing a pretty good job of securing your home every time you went away on vacations in the past. As a matter of fact, one time you even returned from the end of the block just to double check on something because you were worried about leaving so many nice possessions for such a long period of time. But what about short absences?

Regardless of whether you leave house, apartment, farm, or summer cabin, you should take at least some security precautions. Leaving a door or a window open does not only invite the burglar; more important, it makes you vulnerable to surprise attack upon return, since you were so sure that nothing could happen during this brief absence.

After working hard to secure your home, let us not slip up in this department. A knock or ring at the door can determine for the bad guy whether someone is home or not. If no answer, he can safely try the door, and then admit himself. If there is an answer he can always ask for a glass of water or whether the Joneses still live here. Neither gambit makes him a criminal. Incidentally, this knock or ringing of the bell is just as effective in a busy apartment building as it is at a deserted farm.

Regular Trips

A sum as large as $100,000 has hardly ever been stolen from any bank, company, or other organization's safe without prior planning, sometimes months of planning. You don't live in a bank, and hardly ever keep that amount around your home. Yet, if you remember earlier when we discussed some strange formula about risk and return from any given theft, it is quite feasible that a fellow may not want to knock on doors indiscriminately. He may feel that the amount of loot available warrants at least a few days of his valuable time.

It does not take too many days to determine that you leave every morning at 9:10 to put junior safely on the kindergarten bus, and that you have to leave by 4:15 in order to meet Dad at the train in time. To Adolf these would be part of your "regular" trips, would indicate to him about how much time he will have for his job. Don't make life easier for him by rushing out without locking doors and windows.

At the risk of being repetitious, let us emphasize that neither location nor time of day will make any difference. From regular walks with that faithful hound every night after the eleven o'clock news to regular church attendance on Sunday morning or bowling league on Tuesday night—*you would be wise to make everything secure before leaving*.

Irregular Trips

While after the first day of observation, Adolf has a pretty good idea how much time there will be to complete the job when you leave on a regular errand, he does not know how soon you will return from an "unscheduled" one. Therefore, it would seem that he is more likely to strike when he knows about how much time you will allow him. Except for one thing: He also knows that you may be more negligent on that quick run to the store and back; or what started out as only a quick check on the mail downstairs and wound up as a two-hour kaffeeklatsch in apartment 6B. *When leaving your abode, assume that an unauthorized person stands next to you, just waiting to enter.*

Feel you have to leave the door open because the youngest member of the family may return during your absence without a key? No, don't risk belongings and possibly life for that reason. If Junior is old enough, have him wear his own key around his neck to prevent loss, or instruct him to wait at the neighbors' until your return. In case your neighbor does not want *her baby* to let himself into an empty apartment or house, you may explain that the home secured with a key is much safer than the one she left open not only for "baby," but also for every criminal.

Evening Gowns and Bowling Balls

Adolf may feel that proceeds from previous jobs do not warrant an entire week of surveillance, or even one full day, to separate "regular" from "irregular" absences. But even the most casual stroll through a street or an apartment house corridor will sooner or later bring him face to face with a person leaving. He is not in the habit of asking this person, "Will you stay away long?" but he will take another look. His trained eyes will see much more at one glimpse than a beautiful evening gown, or a bowling ball in your hand. There are many more and varied signs that can give him a rather good indication about the length of your absence.

Moral of this chapter then: Don't just look before leaping—*lock before leaving,* not only when you find the time, but always!

-10-

Far Away from Home

Most people spend a fine vacation or two within the continental limits of the United States, before hopping a jet to Timbuctu. But John Doe, our going-to-be world traveler, is leaving for some faraway countries, and has exchanged most of his cash into checks or pieces of paper that do not really look like a good old dollar bill. For some reason, the owner does not respect this loot as he would a bundle of greenbacks.

When John arrives in the country of "Y," he exchanges a portion of his checks into yen, marks, liras, or what have you. Whatever the local currency may be called, whatever it may look like, it just does not feel *right* to this all-American tourist. When spending money in "Y" he gives that polite, sheepish smile which implies: "Sorry to have to give you this garbage, but this is the stuff they gave me at the bank as legal tender."

When leaving this country for the land of "Z," the leftover currency is then changed into still another kind of bargaining material, and therefore becomes even more watered down, more confusing, and worth less in the eyes of our tourist. He thought it possible to live with "Y" money after a relatively short stay, but this "Z" is absolutely impossible.

To make life at least a little easier on himself, he will place the largest of these funny looking bills on the outside of his wad to keep the smaller ones together. True, they are too large to fit into his wallet, but he never bothered to observe the way natives fold these notes of large denomination into quarters to avoid drawing attention.

While paying for his drink, John will display several of these large bills, explaining to the barkeep that these are the funniest pieces of toilet tissue he has ever seen. The bartender needs no explanation, he has not only handled this merchandise all his life, he knows the true value of these bills, and also how hard he has to work to earn just one of them. As a matter of fact, right about now would be time for John to remember that nobody gave him this piece of tissue gratis. While remembering, he also may want to remember this, no matter which country he happens to be in: *Witnesses to his display of paper products are people who are fully aware of the buying power of that amount of cash.*

And of course each country has its share of bad guys. Why should any bad guy gamble on finding only a rubber band, two pennies, and a worthless parimutuel ticket in his victim's pockets when John just proved that he is a truly worthwhile target?

What does John Doe have to do with you? Actually nothing, since you are the careful and sensible type. However, you may do your about-to-leave-by-jet friend a favor by telling him about it, because we have met too many foolish John Does—worldwide.

Conversation With Accent

We agree that you are the person who uses discretion, both in this country and in faraway places. So not even the fellow sitting near you will know exactly how much is left in your pockets after you pay for one drink—but he is still curious, and he has not given up. His "detection device" is friendly, simple, and *apparently innocent* conversation.

It's this conversation we want to warn you about. Only natural that during your vacation you want to have a good time, want to get as much fun and enjoyment as possible, and part of all this is "getting acquainted." But whether the conversation centers around a date for tonight or the location of the best coffeehouse in town, please be on guard. There is no reason to reveal your innermost secrets to every

Gustav, Tokumoto, or Pierre. Remember that one of them may be the fellow who was unable to see the loot, and is now only after information.

This *eager* listener, who may laugh at your jokes a bit too much, does not have to be a mean-looking villain. You may meet a charming couple or a striking redhead. Open season on tourists lasts 365 days each year, and whether you saved all your life to go on this particular trip or it is merely one of many, the chances are excellent that your pocketbook right now contains more than when you visited the local movie at home or shopped for a container of milk at the supermarket. But you did not come with only a pocketbook to this country—what about the rest of your belongings? *Mr. Badguy wants to be convinced that you and your room are worthwhile targets; don't oblige him!*

"Spent my last vacation on our forty-foot yacht" may sound like an innocent statement, since he won't be able to steal or harm this pride of the family, anchored safely in Cold Spring Harbor, U.S.A. But before you have a chance to give him the name of this vessel, he knows that none of the jewelry he will find in your room was bought in the five-and-ten, and although he has never laid eyes on it, he has a good idea that the camera he will find there is not a Brownie box flicker.

Conversation Without Accent

After spending some time in faraway "Z" land, enjoying the scenery and humorous accents of the natives, you may possibly look forward to a quiet chat with one of the many Americans overseas. He is one in the rapidly growing community of friendly United States citizens (with passport to prove it) who has lived in "Z" since World War II days, or since he jumped ship, or since he was hired (then fired) by an American or a foreign firm, and who is now interested only in "showing you a good time." After all, he has lived there all this while, speaks the language of "Z" quite well, knows all the places where the *real* bargains are, and knows where they serve the largest drinks for the least amount of money.

Whether you are interested in bargains or drink is immaterial, this fellow's main attraction lies in the fact that he is a piece of "home," and speaks without an accent. Please don't interpret this to mean that he must be the trustworthy fellow to whom you can reveal your secrets and problems.

Remember that hitchhiker you did not pick up last year back home, because you heeded police warnings about picking up strangers. Well, this is the very same fellow, only he beat you to "Z" by about a year. He has been busy, then hungry, until he finally found his niche in life. He now looks for his prey among the Yankee tourists, knows his value to them, and by now has such a good alibi that only a trained interrogator could break his story.

Why can this fellow become your closest friend in all of "Z" before you even have a chance to buy him a second drink? Circumstances, nothing more.

Our Apologies

At this point we wish to apologize humbly and sincerely to all those who render assistance and advice to tourists everywhere, unselfishly and without ulterior motive; we know only too well that you are there, doing a commendable job. We also admit to one and all that for every "bad apple" we observed over a period of ten years, there were hundreds of helpful folk, with and without accent.

But should serious questions or problems arise, it is good to know that in the Land of Z the entire staff of your nearest embassy, consulate, bank, air or steamship line is prepared to assist you. Even if they themselves cannot solve your problem, let *them* make a few telephone calls for you, so that you do not have to spend a major portion of your vacation trying to get the right party through five switchboards (in a foreign tongue). Go on and sightsee or window-shop while these calls are being made, because in certain countries even a local call may not be completed before you return from a grand tour of the city.

Although you may not speak a single word of "Z," there will normally be enough honest people available to answer routine questions, to engage in some friendly conversation, and even escort you to a fancy nightclub. Among them are the many employees of the United States government or United States firms, members of religious orders, students and businessmen, or right downstairs your own hotel desk clerk.

Pickpockets and the Like

The United States has the tallest buildings and the best baseball players in the world; it does *not* have the most skillful pickpockets. The efficiency, ingenuity, and dexterity of some foreign masters are utterly fantastic and almost unbelievable.

Of course you know that the lazy ones in our country ride public elevators that display a "Caution Pickpockets" sign. As you enter and detect the sign, you automatically reach for the most valuable possession on your person, and pinpoint its location. No, nothing will be taken while riding this elevator because you have pickpockets on your mind. However, two minutes later the sign will be forgotten, and the valuables will be gone.

Overseas experts hardly ever rely on such outside assistance, because in addition to taking the most valuable item, they are able to "clean you out" completely in one simple operation. You will not become aware of anything until you return to your hotel or want to pay the bill at some restaurant. As a tourist you are not only a lucrative target, but you are the person who can often be found in theatres, at horse races, and in bullfight arenas.

Don't stay away from those places—they represent part of your vacation fun. But, *before* the final curtain, the last race or fight, secure all valuables as much as possible, button all buttons, including the top one on your overcoat or jacket. You are about to enter the ideal workshop for pickpockets anywhere: *Large crowds leaving theatres, racetracks, or arenas at the same time through narrow doors and exits.*

The meek and genteel operators will settle for wallets, pocketbooks, and items found in any open pockets in coats, jackets, or trousers; bolder ones are known to have taken or torn off bracelets, watches, and necklaces. You may have seen that rather famous photograph in which a sardine-like crowd leaves the bullring, depicting one "operator" with his arm almost up to the elbow in his neighbor's coat.

Not *all* pickpockets have the price of admission to these events. Some will bump into you in broad daylight, in the middle of the street, and while apologizing will place some of your belongings in their pocket, since the theft has already taken place. It is impossible to detail the thousands of tricks that successful "team" operators have perfected over the years. Let this word of caution guide you: Whether you can understand his language or not, be courteous to that stranger who walks up to you and asks for a light, for directions, or for the right time. But, at the same time, be sure to watch out for any possible number-two man who starts reaching or bumping.

Initially, number one is only there to distract you, but he can also delay you sufficiently should you want to run after number two. Normally, this encounter in the street will not become dangerous for you unless number one "offers his help" to capture number two, because when you catch up with this much-too-clumsy pickpocket in a deserted alley, *both* will strip you of all your belongings, and will carry sufficient armament to make certain they get what they want.

Of course you realize that this teamwork does not apply only to pickpockets. While in the best coffeehouse in town, a distinguished-looking stranger requests permission to sit at your table (*not* an uncommon practice in many parts of the world), and after ten minutes offers you a priceless diamond ring for only $10,000. He confides in you because as a stranger you have no reason to reveal to local folk that his famous family is in financial straits. The restaurant is respectable, the seller looks confident and well groomed, the ring is lovely, and the story plausible. Yet you hesitate to talk business, because you don't know that much about diamonds. "It so happens" that the person at the next table overheard your conversation. He identifies himself as a diamond merchant from Amsterdam, places a jeweler's loupe in his eye to inspect the diamond, and without hesitation offers $50,000 for this "magnificent diamond." A gullible tourist might wind up fighting over the honor of buying a $100 zircon for $10,000.

And just in case you plan to be the seller, because you have depleted your vacation fund or have heard about the easy money which can be made on the black market even today—*don't!* First, if you are not a cheat in the United States, why try your luck so far away from home? Enough of our countrymen have already stuffed newspapers into empty cartons of American cigarettes, sealed them, and sold them at exorbitant prices to innocent foreigners. This practice did not make too many friends overseas. On the other hand, cartons of valuable smokes are being offered every day at dark corners throughout the world by relatively innocent American tourists. The prospective buyer has been known to get a firm grip on his purchase, then, with the other hand reached into his pocket and instead of producing money, come up with a knife with which he slashed the tourist's extended hand, before running away.

Do's and Don't's

No book and no person can prepare you for all the strange situations you may find yourself in when visiting a faraway place. But far or near, we are going to list at least a few observations, some of which may assist on any trip:

DO learn as much as possible beforehand about the place of your visit.

DO learn a few words of the language so you may summon help in an emergency.

DO leave at least some of your jewelry at home.

DON'T carry all of your photographic, electronic, and optical gear through the hotel lobby, casually slung over your shoulder and in full view. Take only what you need for that particular excursion.

DON'T rent the biggest automobile available, unless your family is large.

DON'T leave jewelry and expensive gear in view at *any time* in your room. You may only ask for towels or ice cubes, but *alert eyes come with every order*.

DON'T get careless with greenbacks, just because they are not the local currency. There is no person on earth who is not eager to get his hands on a handful.

DON'T carry all your money in one pocket, but just as important: Don't carry all identification in one wallet or pocketbook.

DO make use of money belt or special garter and, assuming that you stay in reliable accommodations, the hotel safe.

DON'T stray off the beaten path too much by yourself, especially at night.

DO see local, quaint, and hidden places, but make certain that you are with a reliable guide, or at least with a group of people you know.

DO show a certain amount of curiosity, but tempered with proved discretion.

DON'T join groups or parades in the street, no matter how gay they act, without knowing the *reason for the demonstration*. Pickpockets are unpleasant, but angry communist or anti-American mobs can be worse.

DON'T let drink and temptation, coupled with soft moonlight, lead you to just any old broken-down shack.

DO have a good time, but make sure that you and your newly acquired mementos return home safely.

-11-

Hotel/Motel Room

A fresh bed sheet you will get, but don't expect even the fanciest of hotels to change the lock on the door just for you.

Besides the key you now hold, there is one for the maid, one for the floor manager, one at the desk, one for management, one for maintenance crew, house detective, and possibly many more, not counting all those that are either lost or unaccounted for. Yes we know, they don't all look exactly alike, but they all serve to gain entrance to your particular room.

Assuming that each person now employed by the hotel is completely honest and so discreet that he will never even disturb your privacy—that still leaves those who *used to work* at the hotel, those who were fired and possibly had access to master keys, or the local fellow who occupied your fancy suite for one night only, just so that he could make a duplicate key for future reference.

You know all that—that's why you plan to stay in a small and cozy place where the desk clerk on duty knows each guest. But large or small, all have their security problems, and the problem is by no means an easy one. To control the traffic in a large hotel is almost impossible, and even the most reliable desk clerk in a small and cozy place does have to desert his post at times to use the bathroom.

Do we worry, do we fret? Not at all. We just consider that hunk of wood inside the doorframe exactly what it is: A hunk of wood that swings freely for anyone who cares to push it. Knowing and remembering this fact at all times, we will govern our actions accordingly.

Knock, Knock, Who's There?

Remember, at home, when Adolf knocked to determine whether someone was home or not? Well, this method is just as effective here, especially at night. Only *this* knock has an added significance. As you are a tourist, it is understandable that you have had another exhausting day, and for that reason are more soundly asleep than you would normally be at home. Furthermore, the chances are good that faithful Rover did not accompany you, and every burglar alarm which ordinarily would guard your bedroom is not installed here.

Odds: all in his favor. So much so that he can probably come visiting safely while you are asleep.

Without consulting any spy manuals, which allegedly come in certain cereal boxes now, the author would like to list a few tricks that have enabled him to sleep soundly and undisturbed in hundreds of strange rooms throughout the world. Discussion about "secret devices" employed for security will be limited to those found in every hotel room, but we feel certain that you can make use of many other items, and with a bit of ingenuity come up with even better, more sophisticated, and effective ideas of your own.

Have you ever stayed anywhere where you did not find at least one of the following items:

1. Coathanger

2. Chair

3. Drawer.

Now don't go out of your way and spend extra money on overnight accommodations at some fancy place just to get one *each* of the above, because any *one* of them will make an effective security device.

Coathanger

Normally rooms can be locked from the inside. They should be locked with the *key left in the lock*. Trouble is that any amateur can manipulate the key in such a way that it will fall out, thus admitting a passkey or other tool that will open the lock. Since any master keying, necessary in hotels, will weaken lock security, we are not about to expose the open keyhole to anyone. (For latest developments in master keying see Chapter 16.)

Solution: Turn the key as far as it will go toward the locked position, then insert the hanger hook through the hole in the key (or key ring), and hook the hanger over the doorknob.

Some hotels will go to all sorts of trouble to prevent you from "locking yourself in." There may be no keyway at all on the inside, and

A coathanger can secure the key, preventing others from using a passkey.

the only locking bolt you have can be opened with a key from the *outside* only. In that case, we will use our coathanger as a "burglar alarm."

If the door swings in, place a hanger over the top of the doorframe, and attach any handy noisemaker, such as the hotel key. No matter how carefully the door is opened, it will dislodge the hanger and cause it to fall. For greater effect, you can remove the rug; if that is impossible, place an empty suitcase under the "noisemaker" as a soundboard.

If the door swings out, place the hanger over the doorknob, or if possible at a higher place such as molding or between the top of the door and the frame. Keep part of the hanger overlapping the doorframe, so that opening of the door will activate the alarm.

With slight modifications, this principle can be used effectively on almost any window as well as door.

Chair

A chair, with the backrest forced under the doorknob, can make entry rather difficult. Since the chair must lean against the door to be effective, we should prevent the legs from slipping. Wall-to-wall carpeting will serve this purpose very nicely. Where there is no carpeting, the legs can be placed in men's shoes just above the rubber heels, with the toe of the shoe pointing toward the door.

You don't always travel with men's shoes among your baggage? OK then, use overshoes or a nonskid bathmat. None of these items available? Surely you will think of something before you have to utilize your leather gloves as skid prevention.

The traveler can consider himself truly lucky if his door has one of those old-fashioned, and still very much in use, door *handles* instead of knobs. All that is needed here is to prevent the operation of this handle, regardless of lock security. That very same chair can be used most effectively, except that it may rest on all four legs, if so desired, since it will only have to keep the handle in its horizontal position. A telephone directory will serve well to fill any possible space between the handle and the back of the chair.

If you don't feel like using anything as complicated as that, place the chair in front of the door, with the seat facing the room. Now tip the chair against the door in such a way that any movement of the door, in or out, will cause it to fall, especially if the door and the back

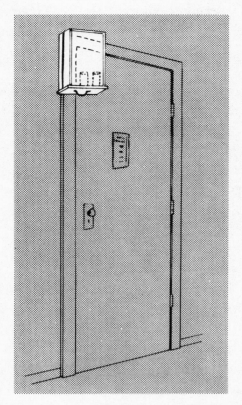

A nightstand drawer, with waterglasses if desired, can become one of many simple but effective "alarms" for your hotel/motel room.

of the chair are not exactly parallel, making the chair "hold on" with only one corner of the backrest.

Drawer

Barricading the door with all available furniture might look quite dramatic in a Western movie; we hardly recommend it for the modern traveler. Instead of taking the entire dresser or nightstand, we suggest the use of a single small drawer out of either one.

If the door opens in, place the corner of the drawer over the upper corner of the doorframe so that the door will dislodge it when opened. If the door swings out, the doorknob will support this drawer until the doorframe makes it fall when the door is operated.

Sound sleeper? Then modify any of the alarm systems. Drawers don't have to be empty. A few water glasses inside the drawer will certainly add to the general commotion. Feel confident that you will sleep through it all, no matter how much noise there is? *Remember that your "visitor" is awake. He will think twice before taking another step.*

He knows that even if this noise did not awaken you or attract hotel personnel, the newlyweds across the hall and the bridge players next door are not asleep yet. They may have been alerted. Since you are obviously not the ordinary John Doe tourist, there is no telling what other surprise you may have in store for him inside. He'll leave and try a safer target.

Your Own Lock

Want to splurge? Invest a few dollars in a portable lock which can be used on almost any door. A variety of this type of lock is now available, and you may want to inspect several to determine which lock will suit your particular purpose. And while inspecting, don't be afraid to hold the lock in your hand; remember, *weight* will enter into the picture at all those places where a redcap is hard to come by (or

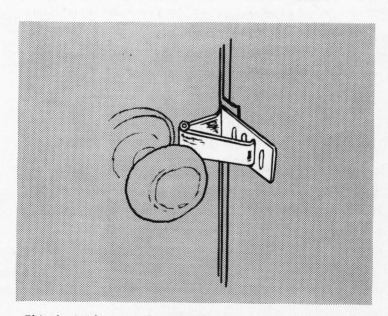

This device keeps a door closed while you are in the room.

when the airline weighs not only all the souvenirs you are bringing back, but also charges extra to transport a heavy security device).

One of the simplest and lightest devices we know of comes in two parts, and has no complicated mechanism of any kind, not even a key. Like the other items mentioned below, no tools or special knowledge is required for installation. This particular unit is effective only if the door opens into the room, but since most hotel/motel doors are mounted to avoid collision with waiters carrying breakfast trays, this characteristic is no great drawback. However, it will not protect the room while you are away, since it can be mounted only from the inside.

A slightly heavier, costlier, and more versatile device comes with lock and key. This unit will not only make it impossible for the door to be operated while you are in the room, but, if so desired, can be used to deny entry to anyone by using the lock and key outside the room when leaving.

By far the smallest and lightest, yet very effective, device is mentioned last, because it can be used only in doors that still utilize the traditional keyhole. The keyhole lock can not only be inserted from either side of the door, but has the advantage of being sealed completely at one end, making it impossible for anyone so inclined to pick while you sleep. We mention this lock here because on your overseas trips you may very well encounter this type of keyhole, also possibly right here in our country, in some quaint, old-fashioned hideaways.

Incidentally, this very same lock can be used most effectively in your summer place, tool shed, barn, warehouse, or any other door

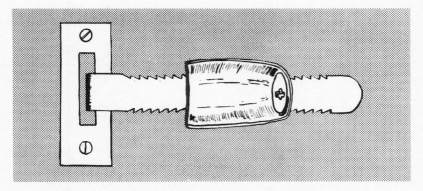

This device can lock the door from inside or outside.

that still employs the type of keyhole described above. Instead of replacing the entire locking mechanism, the keyhole lock can be inserted without tools at a fraction of the cost of replacing the present mechanism.

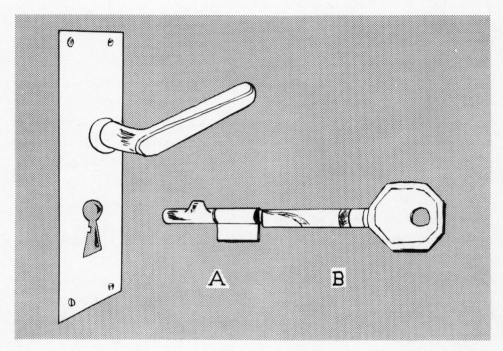

Old-fashioned keyhole becomes quite secure when small lock
(A) is inserted and modern key (B) withdrawn.

-12-

Your Car

More than any other nation in the world, we consider our automobile a necessity rather than a luxury item. We treat it like a comfortable pair of shoes, and use it as our second home. Without regard for safety or security, we park by day or night as close as possible to the door we are about to enter; without regard for protection, we store any and all items inside. We are certain that nobody will do harm to this integral part of our family because it has been registered in our name, carries license plates to prove it, and is obviously our property. But: Your car is not a pair of shoes to the potential thief. Casual inspection will tell him that this is the right type and size of car he wants, he knows that plates can be switched in no time, and that it will become extremely difficult, even for you, to recognize it again once it is painted bright red.

He also knows that this is not a home. It has been left in an area where no friendly neighbors would recognize the owner, and it has been equipped with wheels for easy stealability (not to mention horses under the hood to help in the getaway).

Second Home

You have been warned about leaving valuables in your automobile. You have been particularly cautioned by police not to leave anything of value in plain sight when leaving your auto. Good advice. But don't feel smug about leaving anything in your glove compartment because it can't be seen from outside.

A San Francisco-to-New York well-organized ring of thieves, pickpockets, muggers, and prostitutes made a fortune with their lucrative sideline: selling and renting stolen credit cards through brokers. Their main source of supply: glove compartments. The law moved in on this particular gang early in 1967, but you can be sure another will take its place.

Of course, these crooks did not find a credit card in each car they searched, but they all knew that this little box has become our "safe" away from home, and for that reason were willing to settle for some other article of value. In many cases the card was not missed by the owner for some time, because the open car and unlocked compartment left no signs of possible theft. It is a New York State law that the *"owner of credit card is required to make good any unauthorized purchase unless card was reported stolen."* How about your state?

Until recently, we would have told you to lock anything of value into your automobile trunk, since that is the most secure area available. It still is, except that we must caution you about a group of specialists who can be found in ever-increasing numbers in and around the better resort areas. Their target: the contents of car trunks. Since it is not easy to gain access, they steal automobiles without any intention of ever selling or using them. They drive to a "safe" location, gain access to the trunk by breaking the lock or removing the back seat backrest, help themselves to the valuables, and then abandon the car. Don't try to outsmart these thieves by placing your most valuable necklace inside the well for the spare tire: that is the place where *they* carry burglar tools, narcotics, or other contraband, thinking that no detective will ever look into this hiding place.

Driving

Especially at night, keep your doors locked and your windows up. For fresh air, open the vents under the dashboard, and if you wish, leave each of the windows open just a bit.

On a deserted street, stay in the center as much as you can. If you must stop for a red light, be prepared to go, light or no! We are not, repeat *not*, telling you to run red lights whenever you feel like it. We are saying that in case a person wants to attack you or enter your automobile, the easiest defense is to be ready to move. Of course, you must use caution, must watch for other traffic, but we are talking about a deserted area. If you don't want to take a chance crossing the intersection, make a right turn, which will be in the direction of any possible moving traffic. Worried about a traffic violation for running a red light? Don't be; while running this light, lean on your horn and hope for some nice policeman to come to your rescue.

And speaking of nice policemen, the official advice from the Department in case your car breaks down at night: *Pull to the side of the road, lock yourself in, and display a white cloth or marker from the driver's window.*

Parking

If your child took his new toy, willfully threw it into a pond, and then asked you to recover it, would you? No, not a strange question at all. Hundreds and hundreds of motorists leave their "toys" parked somewhere every day, and willfully leave the key in the ignition for anyone to use. Yet, when someone does, they have the audacity to expect someone else to jump into the pond and recover it!

Insurance rates must go up because of this practice, policemen and innocent bystanders will get hurt while the car is being chased, and some relatively innocent youngster will get a black mark on his record when he gets caught. Statistics show that over 60 percent of cars reported stolen were taken by youngsters under the age of eighteen. Many only "borrowed" the car for a short time when the key in the ignition proved too great a temptation. Please warn your own children that this kind of joyride is considered a felony, and can bring up to ten years in jail—despite the fact that some idiot of an adult left an open invitation.

In case removal of the key becomes too much of a burden for you, purchase one of several inexpensive, spring-loaded gadgets which will automatically retract the key when the ignition is turned off. Caution: Make sure that the switch is in the *locked* position, not only *off*.

Not too many people leave their key in the ignition while on a long vacation trip, perhaps in the fear of having to walk home. But take a good look at the local supermarket or shopping center parking lot. Not only is the key to the house on that same key ring, but a letter, magazine, or some other document in the car shows the owner's home address. Why should the thief steal only your car, when your house is located on his way home? Besides, not even the most observant neighbor is going to be alarmed when your own car drives into the driveway, and some fellow lets himself in with the proper key.

He may not be in the used car business, but may specialize in looting homes. In that case, he will take only key and address, and possibly leave you with a flat tire so that you will not start for home too soon (providing you carry a spare key). But even if you do start for home, he has bolted the front door from the inside, and will have ample time to depart at his leisure through the back, while you still wonder what happened to the keys.

But your friend has always left *her* keys while shopping "right around home," and nothing ever happened! Well, we do hope she does not get hurt on the night when the fellow who made a wax impression of all her keys for future reference returns. He will enter her home on the night he feels is right, will let himself in with his duplicate key, take the things he wants, load them into *her* car, and drive off.

If at all possible, don't leave *any* key for the cowboy who squeezes your car into a much-too-small spot at a guarded parking lot downtown. If you must leave ignition key, don't leave others on the ring. Don't forget, cowboys can read too, and may have friends who are willing to visit your home, armed with your own key, while the car remains in downtown corral. Should you decide to return early, the cowboy can warn his friend by calling your home.

Parking?

The situation is quite different on a warm summer night, with the moon just right. You may want to park in a quiet spot in order to whisper sweet nothings into your copilot's ear. You two want privacy, you want to be left alone. Don't expect us to interfere, we just want to be helpful.

That lovers' lane in your vicinity may be romantic, may be secluded, but how safe is it from sudden attack? Too much has happened to pilots and copilots at the hands of some enemy of cupid who suddenly pounced on his victims from a bush alongside the car. Don't *ever* drive deep into the woods to get away from it all, don't ever place your car alongside any thick underbrush. Keep a sufficient area of clear visibility around your car at all times. True, others will see your car, but you can take appropriate action before they ever reach you. In case a shady-looking character approaches, drive off.

Returning Home

Earlier in this book we warned you about entering dark, presumably empty or deserted rooms and houses without sufficient caution. This second home is no different. If nothing else, at least look inside the passenger compartment before entering your car. There could be someone stretched out on the floor between the front and back seat. If there is, let's find out *now,* not while driving in the middle of nowhere.

In case it was absolutely necessary to leave your car in a dark section of an undesirable area, be extra careful. For any number of reasons, your car may be singled out as a target by pranksters, gangsters, or the local gang. Yours may be the only car less than ten years old, yours may be the only car that has been washed during the last ten weeks, yours may be the only car, period. Should you notice anything suspicious in or near your car when approaching it, walk past it, try to observe as much as you can, even from across the street. If all seems well upon your return, have the key ready, check inside, get in, and go quickly on your way.

If there is really something wrong, somebody inside your car, or a nasty-looking, boisterous, tough group shouting insults, and just waiting to start a good fight with you, then keep on going and make your call to the local police or sheriff.

You may return and find one or more flat tires. You may even see the valve next to the wheel, proof positive that this is not a normal flat. *Don't make a fist, don't invite the culprit to a fight in the street, and don't start bending down to fix the flat.* At least don't start any of these actions until you have looked around sufficiently to see whether there are one, two, or three strong-armed thugs standing in each of the doorways, waiting to have a good time at your expense. They may not be satisfied to see your nose bleeding, they may want the last greenback out of your wallet and/or pocketbook as well. If you do not want to call the police, at least call a service station to change the wheel for you so that you do not have to face the gang alone.

Protective Devices

If you are one of those persons who normally leaves his key in the ignition while gone, then don't spend one red cent on any device. You would be wasting your money. If you are the careful type, you will always close windows, lock doors, and, of course, take the ignition key with you. You will do this not only if you are the careful type, but also if you are smart enough to realize that your insurance company will not reimburse you for items stolen out of your car unless there are signs of *forcible* entry.

You may want to keep a sturdy flashlight right under or near the front seat. In case somebody tries to slide in after you when entering the car, this light can become a handy weapon. No, do not keep your favorite small weapon in the glove compartment. Even if it has not been stolen by the time you need it (and could then be used against you), it will be too far out of your reach in an emergency.

Devices specifically designed for automobiles are numerous. Among the mechanical ones are locks that will secure the hood, preventing the common practice of crossing ignition wires near the motor. Other locks are designed to forestall the theft of hubcaps, of gas cap (and gas), or prevent the steering wheel from being turned. Among electrical devices are complete alarm systems which will sound a horn, siren, or other noisemaker in case doors, hood, or trunk are being opened while the car is unattended.

Some of these systems can be activated by the driver from inside the car, should he be attacked or be in some other danger. We spoke to the inventor of one of these alarms, and he felt that his own wife, in case of attack, would shut off this system should her attacker demand silence while threatening her with a gun or knife. To avoid this situation, he designed his system in such a way that once it has been activated, it can be turned off only from under the hood with the proper key. Our suggestion: *Place a large sign inside car, in prominent location, stating that alarm is not under driver control, so that the person being threatened can point to this sign without suffering unnecessarily.*

Before buying anything, read the accompanying instructions or, in the case of an entire alarm system, try to get a demonstration. Just as for home devices, here too, make certain that you get the device you really want.

Certain alarms, like some which are offered for the home, depend on proximity, that is, anyone's approach will set off the alarm. Will the car that parks close behind you set it off, or will it be activated only by someone coming too close to one of the locks? Will the alarm turn itself off after so many minutes (sufficient to scare thieves), and then reset itself for the next attempt, or will you come back to a dead battery when returning from the office on the 6:05? Will you have to get your fingers dirty under the hood or under the car to activate this gadget, or will a key-operated separate switch do the job? Give thought to your particular situation and your normal use of car before making any purchase.

-13-

Being Followed?

Earlier in this book we spoke of fear. Here we would like to tackle the specific fear of being followed. More and more of our good up- standing citizens are being afflicted not by concern but by a genuine *obsession* about being followed. Whether more blood-curdling detec- tive stories, more publicity about investigative methods, more late, late movies, or the general increase in crime is responsible, we do not know. What we care about is to make you realize that you are *not* being followed from birth to grave, that your chances of ever being "tailed" are extremely remote, and finally, if you are fairly certain of having a shadow following you, just what you can do.

You are not particularly afraid of anything. You are certainly not obsessed by any particular fear. Yet, somewhere in our lives can come a time when for some specific reason or some peculiar circum- stance (known only to ourselves), we have occasion to believe that someone might just possibly make an attempt at following us. Yes, we said *make an attempt* at following us. This sport of tailing someone is not half as easy as it sounds, and unless you have tried it yourself, you will never know how impossible it can get at times, even for short periods.

Follow the Leader

Next time you get to the office or hairdresser a bit too early and have about ten minutes to kill, conduct the following experiment: Completely at random, pick any person who happens to be in the street. Male, female, young or old, short or tall, makes no difference. Check your watch, and try to follow this person at a discreet distance so that in ten minutes from now that same person is still in your sight.

If indeed you succeeded in following for the entire ten minutes, pat yourself on the back for a job well done—and recall the numerous times during which the quarry almost managed to elude your searching eyes. It wasn't easy, was it? In the event that you selected a nine-foot green-haired giant, remember that since you are neither nine feet tall nor have green hair, it would be an entirely different story if someone wanted to follow you.

In case you lost sight of your suspect after a minute or two, *don't feel bad*. You are not trained in these matters, and therefore cannot be expected to be successful in your first experiment. Yet even if that no-goodnick who might be trailing you has played this game for years, he still has a mighty rough time staying with you: It is an extremely difficult game.

Furthermore, you are not terribly worried about anyone who might possibly be following you through busy downtown streets. You will no doubt feel greater concern if this person attempts to follow you into an elevator, a deserted street, or possibly your own home.

First Things First

Before you start to wipe the perspiration off your forehead, begin to scream, and race breathlessly into the nearest police station, let us make reasonably certain that there is such a thing as a tail following you. Let us make this determination *before* you enter the elevator, *before* you turn into that deserted street, and *before* you reach the door to your own home.

Let's assume that for one reason or other you suspect the fellow in the black hat of following you. Whatever you do, don't panic and don't run. Instead, stop right where you are for what would appear to anyone else a perfectly good reason, such as tying your shoelace, fumbling in your purse for something, buying a paper (after searching for coins in various pockets), getting a shine, or whatever excuse might be handy out there in the street.

If the black hat just passes you by and keeps on walking, you may continue, at a slower pace, *behind* him, long enough to determine that he is really just another pedestrian.

In case the black hat stops near where you are now, *return in the direction you just came from,* walk right past him, if he happens to be on your side of the street, and then stop in front of the largest showcase you can find. Pick one that reflects the traffic on the road well, if possible. You picked a large window because it will not only show what passes directly behind you, but if you stand at one side, the angle of observation will take in quite a stretch of sidewalk to either side of the store. The small window leading to the door, at a 45- or 90-degree angle to the street, may serve your purpose even better.

You see the black hat reflected in the window, and if it disappears as this fellow continues on his original course, that is another good indication that it was not really you he had in mind.

If, on the other hand, this character now comes in your direction *he* must have reversed his course too, and this could just be a wee bit suspicious. Don't run, but at a rather brisk pace walk without stopping or lingering anywhere, all the way to the end of the block, giving anyone who might possibly be following the impression that you are really trying to get away from him (which of course you are). If indeed this character does not want to lose you, he just "got the message" and will quicken his pace.

Without slowing down, turn the corner. Immediately after you are out of black hat's vision, walk slowly up against the wall of the building you just turned and stay put. You may tighten those shoelaces again, or whatever. The important thing here is that black hat's actions on this very corner will tell you with reasonable certainty whether he is interested in shadowing you.

It could just have been a coincidence that this fellow first went up the same block you did, and now walks slowly back this same street. If so, he will pass your "hiding place" without hesitation and continue on his way, disappearing in the crowd. The person who tried to follow you will have quickened his pace, and if he noticed you turn the corner, will immediately do the same. As he looks down the sidewalk, about the distance at which he has been following, he discovers that you are gone and he might well start running, trying to catch up.

Sounds impossible that he will not see you right there, leaning against the building? The explanation is very simple: You did the *unexpected,* since a person under these circumstances is expected to keep on running.

The possibility exists that he never got a chance to see you turn that corner. In that case he will arrive, at a fast pace, and suddenly look in all three directions as bewildered as a four-year-old who lost his mother in the supermarket. There, the chances are good that in his haste he will take off in any direction (following someone he thinks is you), without ever spotting you, and without you ever seeing him again. If, for some reason, he discovers you after giving a very strange performance at this corner, it is time for us to decide on a course of action, since this bloke has used up his chances of "coincidences."

Shake Him

Just shake him off your trail. Difficult? Not if you remember our ten-minute experiment, where you followed a perfectly unaware person who in no way was trying to evade you, but was going about his normal business.

As we are still downtown, you may head for the nearest place where it is safe to assume a lot of people can be found, such as a railroad station, bus terminal, hotel, or large department store. Since it is almost impossible to keep tabs on a person in these places, the black hat may patiently wait for your return at the entrance. Solution: Don't exit through the same door you used to enter this place.

No crowded place nearby? You could consider taking the bus or trolley for just a stop or two. Get on just as either one is ready to pull away from the scheduled stop. In case our friend manages to get on too, sit down (providing there is a spot available for you), and don't get up until the vehicle is about to pull away from the next stop, then make a hasty exit. This game can be played even more effectively in subways, where doors normally close automatically, but for various and sundry reasons, we don't suggest the use of subways for the purpose of "playing games."

No bus, no trolley? Then wait at the nearest intersection until the traffic light is just about ready to turn red, then hurry across the street. With a bit of luck you may be able to see the black hat, with head inside, pinned to the road by a 600 x 16 tire. Or your pursuer may figure out the one prudent thing to do, and that is to wait until the light changes—even at the expense of losing you. And the time lapse will give you the opportunity to get away for good.

On the other hand, he may be a feeble-brained, lucky so-and-so who took a chance and made it safely to your side of the street. At this point you become sick and tired of playing games. What you want right here and now is *help*. Any one of the small police "call boxes," which are enclosed phones connected directly into the nearest precinct, can bring help within seconds. True, these boxes were placed in the street for fast and easy communication between a patrolman and his precinct house, but nobody will object if you make use of one in your present situation.

Of course you did not even have to engage in the very first, or any subsequent segment of this game. You could have started immediately after his corner performance to head for the nearest police precinct or uniformed policeman. But: Since so often neither is within arm's length, you may just want to try one of the above tricks *while on your way to summon help.*

Help!

Please note: This is an appeal for help with only one exclamation point. Nobody has touched you, attacked you, or even threatened you at this point. You are concerned, and rightly so, but don't lose your head, not now, or ever.

When making your report to Officer Murphy on the corner or to the desk sergeant, try to be as calm as possible, and try to give in as few words as possible the facts about what happened to you *just now,* and just why you have reason to believe that you are being followed.

Of course, this is what you were going to do anyway, yet we felt it was worth a reminder. Amazing how many crimes could be solved, hot pursuits started, or arrests made if it were not for the tremendous time lapse between a victim's breathless arrival and the end of his story. We use the word "story" advisedly, because too often it starts with a lecture on nobody being safe in the city; from there it covers some complaints about general police procedure and why don't they ever . . . instead of . . ., etc.; touches lightly on Cousin Charley's identical incident which happened less than a year ago in Brooklyn, and then, only then, will we finally get around to finding out what happened *just now*. No policeman, no squad car, and no law enforcement agency can act quickly unless they are appraised of the situation in a minimum of time. Do come up for air long enough to listen to that pertinent question, while giving your concise report.

As mad, as disgusted, and as frightened as you may be, while on your way to report a crime, it would be worth the effort to push back thoughts about how many days it will take your nose to heal, how much it will cost to replace that heirloom, or how you will ever explain this incident at home. Instead, make an attempt to recall what *really* happened. Who did what to whom? Where? What about that license plate? Did he have dark hair or was it no hair at all? Was that a girl in the doorway, or was it a fellow with real long hair?

Help?

Remember farther back in this chapter when you first became suspicious about the black hat?

Let us assume that you got that certain feeling about being followed when you happened to be fairly near a policeman or you did not feel like "playing games" while on your way to seek help. Yet you really can't be certain about being followed and may not want to appear a fool reporting only a hunch. Hence, "help with a question mark."

Walk right up to Officer Murphy, and while looking straight at the black hat point your finger at this possible tail, asking Murphy: "Is this the general direction of the railroad station" or whatever excuse you may want to use. Of course, you won't raise your voice so that the words will drift clearly under that hat we have been worried about.

Put yourself in the shoes that go with the hat in question. Wouldn't it discourage you from following a person if he very boldly, only a few feet from you and for all the world to see, pointed you out to a policeman? On the other hand, if this hat belonged to just another pedestrian, he might not even notice your gesture or conversation. Furthermore he couldn't care less.

The precinct house happens to be close? Make sure your possible tail sees you enter. Once inside, there must be somebody to give you the correct time, the best way to get to the bus terminal, or directions to the best steak house in town.

Right you are, we are engaging in psychological warfare with our (possible) opponent, and *his own guilt feelings will be his downfall—* and don't say that it won't work! Some of the most vicious criminals, some of the best trained spies in the world, have been caught, trapped, and hanged because they fell for even simpler tricks than the ones mentioned above.

Language Is No Barrier

All right, you say to yourself, maybe this warfare business has some merit, might even try it myself, should the occasion arise. But what about all those faraway places we plan to visit next year. Not only do none of us speak (or understand) a word of the language, we feel those are the places we *really* may need protection.

All we can say to that is, try to remember the last time you committed a "crime" like stepping on someone's freshly seeded lawn, or spilling the ashes on a pretty rug. Remember that accusing finger which pointed at you and singled you out from all the others present? You understood the gesture—not a word had to be spoken.

Lucky for us, this accusing finger means the same in any language, and furthermore is understood real loud and clear by all the peoples of the world. As for your actual conversation with that policeman, it matters very little, as long as you only want to get rid of a black hat that may be following you.

What *will* have a bearing on your efforts is the fact that you are addressing by error a streetcar conductor on his way home, or a mild-mannered mailman who just completed his rounds. Although *you* may not know the difference between one uniform or another, neither of these get-ups is likely to instill fear in the black soul of your shadow.

You would be wise to find out what a policeman's uniform looks like *before* you need one. You might even want to spend an extra minute or two to discover that the Chinese cop in Hong Kong will answer you in perfect English, *if* you locate one who wears that special doodad on his shoulder straps; that a cop in the country you are visiting will not have the same headgear *off* duty as the high and easy-to-spot type he wears while *on* duty; or that even in the remotest

village of Japan you are never more than one block from a police
box, manned by the officer responsible for that particular area.

-14-

Being Overheard?

We did our best to assure you that the chances of being followed from birth to grave are extremely remote. Here we would like to put you at ease by stating that as the "average" citizen (if there is such a person), your home is in all probability not bugged with electronic devices, and no big ears are glued to any of your windows. But in our effort to assist in every way, we do want to point out that in the life of any person there can come a time when he is involved in divorce proceedings, in a land deal, in the acquisition of a new firm, in the development of a new chemical process, in labor-management negotiations, or knows about the length of next year's hemline.

Should these, or similar involvements, strike a familiar note in your ears, it means that at this time you have information which is of value to a third party. Depending on the size of the deal, or alimony, or acreage, this information can be worth thousands of dollars, which would certainly make it worth somebody's while to spend time and effort to eavesdrop.

Had this book been written only a few months ago, there would have been no reference to this type of activity at all. But today you, your neighbor, your worst enemy, and the biggest crook in town can either by mail, or with cash, procure hundreds of effective listening devices that will do a job and do it well. He will *not* need identification, he will *not* have to state the reason for his purchase, and he will *not* have to produce any kind of certificate or license. The only thing he needs is sufficient funds. Frightening?

Measures and Countermeasures

Yes, it is frightening, especially when you consider that most of these devices are so small that it is difficult to detect them, and when hidden properly, detection becomes almost impossible, even for experts in the field.

Before becoming too frightened, let us handle this problem exactly like all others we have encountered so far. Let us put ourselves in the shoes of that wealthy fellow who just purchased the most expensive and most sophisticated of all listening devices; let us remember that for every crooked measure there is a countermeasure, and that we don't want you to spend money unnecessarily.

We urge you, first, if at all possible, never to use a phone, intercom, radio, or other type of communication system to discuss your secrets with anyone (even if you now have a "foolproof" privacy gadget on this equipment).

As the fellow who purchased all the expensive equipment, you would no doubt want to place your devices in those places where your "victim" not only spends most of his time, but where he does most of his talking. Some of the logical places would be in or near the phone; behind, under, or in the living-room couch, or maybe inside his automobile where he will feel secure from eavesdroppers (while you could listen to his every word while following in another car at a safe distance). Placing these miniature transmitters inside homes and cars is no great trick, since they no longer require wires or lengthy antennas.

One of the most effective countermeasures against any listening device is to prevent its introduction into the house in the first place. Reading the previous pages about sly Cousin Benito, about visitor control and escort service again, this time with listening devices in mind, would certainly help. But what if the bugs are already in your home? In that case you could go out to purchase electronic equipment that is twice as powerful, twice as effective, and twice as expensive as all the bugs that may be in your home. Don't! Although your investment *might* succeed in blocking, drowning out, or detecting all bugs, we have much cheaper methods in mind.

Before the secrets of our nation are discussed anywhere, even relatively safe and secure conference rooms are "swept" electronically and double-checked by experts prior to important meetings. Because of circumstances beyond its control, one of these teams of experts could not reach a conference site in time. The conference was not postponed, but instead took place in one of the safest locations possible, the middle of an open field. Why not carry on *your* highly sensitive conversation with lawyer, inventor, or partner while taking a stroll in the park or down the street? Before taking this walk, you might want to check that nobody planted one of these tiny transmitters in your or your partner's pockets or briefcase.

It is raining and you don't feel like getting wet? Then carry on your conversation only in those places where nobody would expect you to discuss important matters: The attic, the basement, the laundry room will all do nicely.

Away from home, in hotel or motel room, turn the radio or TV sound volume up fairly high while keeping your own voices down. In case management furnished neither one of these noisemakers, open water faucet and shower wide. Don't use that plush office at your place of business, but walk over to the shipping department or go into the plant and stand fairly near moving machinery. Warning: Don't make a habit of using any *one* of the above named locations in your home, or *one* special spot in your plant, with such regularity that it becomes known as your "conference room."

Free Consultation

Dear Mr. Chairman of the Board: Do we detect a smirk on your face as you visualize those sixteen distinguished gentlemen who will be at your next meeting standing out there in the plant between drive shafts and transmission gears? May we first assure you that *this* book was not written with you in mind. But just because all the advice on these pages is geared to the individual family and the individual entrepreneur does not mean the biggest of our industrial giants can't benefit.

To do the unexpected can be as effective for one as for seventeen.

To move the location for your once-a-year hush-hush conference might be a good idea, but even a *routine* meeting of this size with your top executives might make you the target for bugging artists. Were the new location of your meeting site known to the competition days or weeks ahead of time, they could take appropriate action, and have the bugs in place with time to spare. Therefore, don't make reservations in your or your firm's name and don't make the reservations for a "conference." Have your private secretary reserve the bridal suite in her and her make-believe husband's name at some good hotel. As you march in with the other sixteen gentlemen, place a fair-sized bill in the bellhop's hand. This will help him to close his wide-open jaws, and will get a few extra chairs into the rooms. You don't care for brides and honeymoons? Then plan a "recital" at one of the local theatres, and have your members of the board occupy orchestra seats in the very center of the theatre. No, this will not cost too much, since no performance is scheduled at this time, and for realism you can invite your daughter to pound the piano while the meeting is in progress. Either location is probably safer than your own conference room for discussing future taillight location or that big advertising campaign you plan for next year.

It goes without saying that neither you nor your secretary (the only two persons to know about this plan, unless you have a security officer who should be told) will discuss details with anyone. Your conference room will be prepared as usual, with seventeen chairs and seventeen ashtrays. Notifications to members of the board will go out as in the past, asking them to attend the yearly conference which will start in your conference room promptly at ten o'clock. The meeting *will* start at the appointed time and place, but will last only long enough to inform everyone present to take a seat in one of the three limousines that are waiting outside. Neither chauffeurs nor guests have to know the exact destination until the cars are ready to leave. (No, next year's meeting will *not* be in the same location.)

Why this chapter in a book about criminals? Because the criminal now has easy access to these sophisticated devices, and will not hesitate to use them, while law enforcement agencies and respectable investigators are restricted in the use of this equipment through legislation—and therefore can be of only limited help to you in matters pertaining to eavesdropping.

-15-

Self-Defense

This brief chapter is most certainly not intended to serve as a substitute for a course given by competent instructors in a reliable school for self-defense. The methods suggested here are a potpourri of those used by the first Japanese to "chop wood" with bare hands, the first knight to unsaddle an opponent, the first instructor to deposit the author on a gym floor, and finally those the author has devised himself. Instead of describing in detail variations in hundreds of techniques, let us concentrate on the one common denominator—an aggressive attacker—and discover how to take advantage of his weak points effectively.

Child's Play

A place called Laos, Southeast Asia, is not located on Santa Claus's scheduled run. No doubt that was the reason why the author could observe ten-year-old natives playing for hours with deadly snakes instead of baseballs.

Not too far from there, in Bangkok, Thailand, the author had occasion to watch doctors and their helpers "milk" and then force-feed extremely poisonous cobras on a snake farm where venom is extracted for serum. In addition to having sharp fangs, some of the slippery inmates are king cobras of such gigantic size and power that it is difficult to understand how either doctor or attendant can live through even one single operation. Yet they do, and they will still be there when you get a chance to visit. Incidentally, don't expect neat cages for each one or two of the inmates; there are hundreds kept in enclosures the size of a basketball court and to feed or milk them means walking inside and picking them up, one at a time!

Protective devices of any kind are nonexistent for the playful children as well as the doctors and attendants; their only handling instruments are bare hands. As a matter of fact, the only difference we detected was that those "on the farm" normally wore regular shoes, while kids played their games barefoot.

Jungles

Why this long tale about snakes? For a twofold purpose: It is believed that, besides the author, there are quite a number of persons who avoid, fear, and possibly even hate snakes more than any other creatures on earth. Furthermore we feel that no kid on Forty-second Street, no machine-gun-carrying Chicago gangster, and no Pacific waterfront tough-guy can be faster, nastier, or more deadly than a hungry snake.

If those people can learn not only to cope with, but to *live with,* the greatest danger in their part of the world, should we not be able to defend ourselves against the most ferocious species in our asphalt and concrete jungle?

Why are the inhabitants of the green jungle so successful? Simple. They have found their opponents' weakest point, know its exact location, know how to reach it quickly and with confidence in order to become masters of the situation.

Since the beast in our jungle claims to be a higher form of animal life, he also has to contend with more vulnerable areas, such as nerve centers and pressure points. Let's go after those weak points of his, and see if we can't make him behave.

Snakes

A closer inspection of our concrete-jungle snake-in-the-grass reveals that he has so many Achilles' heels that it would be downright confusing to mention all. Instead, let us concentrate on some of the most important of his vulnerable spots, let us remember them, and let us get there quickly in time of need.

Severe pressure on any of these points will make him squirm, a sharp blow in the same places will send him crawling back into his hole.

Note, we spoke of *severe* pressure and *sharp* blows. In order to make whatever force you can muster more effective, reduce to a minimum the area through which this force is being delivered. What do we mean? Simply this: The force your fist can deliver is spread over a relatively large area. This same force can be much more effective when delivered by one single knuckle.

Want proof? Apply pressure to any of your own nerve centers with your fist. Now, instead of the entire fist, use only the *center* knuckle of your middle finger, which you extend slightly, so that it can be held firmly in place by the adjacent fingers. Apply the same amount of pressure, and note the difference.

Some people become proficient in delivering jabs with only the tips of their fingers, while keeping hand and fingers straight, slightly cupped. This thrust, if executed correctly, can be quite effective.

The most customary application of the reduced-area principle is commonly referred to as the judo and or karate chop, where the blow is delivered by the edge of an open hand. Experts at this can actually break a wooden board in half. Our humble suggestion: Don't try chopping wood without a certain amount of practice; it can hurt.

Practice? When? These days, when there seems to be not even time for a quiet meal, most of us are not favorably inclined to take on another time-consuming chore of any kind. Yet you can become quite accomplished by merely striking nearby objects with the edge of your hand, while going about the everyday routine. Indoors, refrigerator and doors can become handy targets, while outdoors, buildings or fenceposts may serve as targets as you pass them.

(Incidentally, since this practice can go on while walking home through a deserted street, do you suppose it could have a certain effect on a fellow following you, who had his eyes on your pocketbook? Strike a mailbox or similar noisy object. That ought to shake him up!)

In addition to hands, we have quite a versatile defense mechanism in our feet, and enough weak points in our opponent are located low enough for easy reach. These feet can be quite devastating, with or without high heels, especially against any attack from the rear. Many a strong fighter has been defeated by the clever use of "foot punches," which are legal in Thai boxing.

Ever thought of using your elbows? Either one can do a good job against attack from side or rear. Although they are shaped just right for our purpose, few people ever make use of them.

Built-ins

Last, but by no means least of the built-in defenses, is your voice. It is as good as an alarm system to summon help, and should be used for that reason. But here we have something more important in mind. With every blow you deliver, scream! We don't mean yell for help but scream at the top of your lungs as though your life depended on it.

From what the big boys tell us, this can do much more than bring help. It will serve all of the following purposes:

1. Scare your opponent.

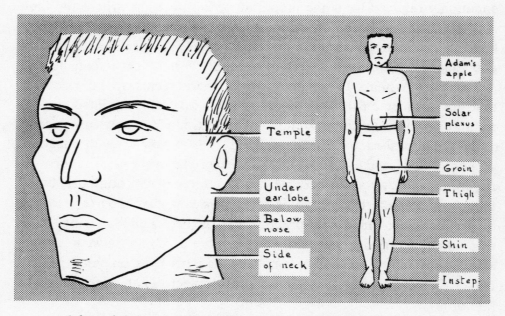

A few of the many vulnerable spots on an attacker's head, and on his body.

2. Help tighten your own body in preparation for the blow you are about to deliver.

3. Help convince yourself that you are bigger, stronger, braver than you thought.

Don't feel foolish or shy about making use of this gruesome noise. Attacking Indians, jumping parachutists, and even cornered lions never hesitate to make full use of *their* vocal cords.

Caution!

We will briefly cover a few of the innumerable man-made gadgets and devices that fall into the self-defense category. Before we do, *a word of warning which should not be taken lightly.*

Is the device legal in your state and community?
Is it kept out of reach of children?
Are you completely familiar with its function and use?

Legal: You are aware that the mere possession of a firearm might be illegal in your state unless you are licensed. Are you aware that there are laws against the use of certain gases, even if carried in a tiny fountain-pen-type container, strictly for self-defense? The sling-shot you used as a kid has been declared illegal in some states. Better check before you buy or use a gadget.

But even without a weapon of any kind in your hand, the law has much to say about self-defense. Since it is impossible to cover all the ramifications here, the author would like to quote his favorite professor, Dr. Robert E. Stone, who had the following to say about this complicated and involved subject:

"There is law on this subject that ought to be taught, but the danger in teaching is that students may be led thereby to assert their rights to use force when such is not absolutely necessary. A person may use all force necessary to protect himself. This is known as self-defense, and in its execution one may take life. However, if his own safety can be preserved by retreating, he must do so rather than take life. But if the assault is in his home, or if retreat would be dangerous and the best defense is an offense, he is entitled to attack. If the assailant at any time starts to retreat, then the one attacked must cease the use of force.

"If the attack is obviously not of a fatal or overly serious nature, one is not entitled to kill the attacker. In other words, one may resist force with force, to any degree necessary to repel an attack, but the extent of the force must be limited to acts short of killing except where one's life or serious bodily injury is at stake.

"In no event is one entitled to kill merely to protect property. But one may take almost any steps to resist a *robbery*. The victim may strike with his fist, hit with a club, or shoot. It makes no difference whether the property attempted to be taken is of trifling value. In one's own home, or even in a private place of business, one may keep out intruders and eject those that are within. Here again the amount of force to be used must not exceed that which is reasonable and necessary."

Reach: Please make certain that the device you purchased for defense does not instead become the source of grief in your own home. Of course that firearm will be in a safe place, but are you aware that children have been blinded while inspecting gas containers which to them looked like lipsticks?

Use: Make sure you not only get to the fine print of the instruction sheet that came with the device, but also *read this fine print with special attention*. Before you were licensed for that pistol, somebody checked that you were not a convicted criminal; nobody seemed to care whether you knew how to use this weapon. Of course this makes no difference in your case, since membership in a pistol club, hunting trips, and prior service in one branch of the armed forces has familiarized you completely with guns. But did you ever use a firearm *at close quarters?* If not, you have watched enough movies, television shows, and stage productions to be completely familiar with the scene. Incredible as it sounds, good and bad guy alike will walk right up to his opponent with gun extended as though he were on the pistol range, aiming at a target over a hundred feet away. Don't you follow their example! Don't get so close to your opponent that he can reach you. Keep your bent elbow comfortably alongside and slightly *back* of your body while your forearm helps to point the weapon. Keep the gun in this position. If you must fire, do it from this position, since your free arm can keep your opponent from deflecting or grabbing your artillery, should he lunge forward.

Pennies, Nickels, and Dimes

Meanwhile, back at the jungle, all those weak points in our attacker are still waiting for further attention. For lack of strength, or lack of confidence, you feel that a blow delivered by you will not be sufficient, even if previously described methods are used.

Care to add some impetus to your punch?

Banks do a wonderful job of wrapping pennies, nickels, and dimes. The size of one of these rolls is sure to fit comfortably into your hand, and it is amazing what this can do to your striking power. However, aside from "tying up capital," these coins also present a weight problem, if they are to become your constant companion. For that reason we recommend the use of a stick.

The type of stick we have in mind has been used as successfully by burly British commandos as by the smallest Oriental. This simple device comes in various lengths, is known by many names, and because of its effectiveness is being marketed commercially. Shaped like one of the rolls of coins above, it is longer. The protruding portions at either end, jutting out from your fist, can be used either to strike a blow or to apply pressure to the most conveniently located sensitive area, should a "snake" try to envelop you.

In choosing this type of weapon, don't try to get as much wood as possible for your money. An eight-inch or longer gadget can too easily be wrestled out of your hand.

There are many ways in which this innocent-looking stick can be used or held, but for the purpose of this discussion: Hold the stick firmly in a tight fist. This enables you to strike in all directions with either of the protruding ends.

When taking this particular weapon to faraway countries, the cus-

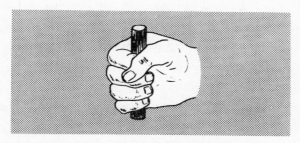

A short simple stick can be very effective.

toms official will not ask you to declare it or to produce a license for its use.

Guns, Gas, and Gadgets

Because some people want more than a stick in their hand, the old brass knuckles, blackjacks, and even nightsticks or billy clubs have made their appearance in new, twentieth-century editions. Clubs can be had which impart an electric shock or, if you prefer, light your way home with their own power source. The judge who hears the case, after you successfully defend yourself against attack, may well make a great distinction between having *repelled an intruder* with one of these items, or having "carried a concealed weapon" while on the town. Better check local laws first. Using an umbrella (especially the folding kind), tightly rolled newspaper, or one of the four corners of this book in self-defense should not upset even the strictest guardian of our judiciary system.

Since all human animals will be thrown off balance by anything which might be hurled into their faces, the small dispensers of certain gas or liquid have become popular. Although some may not be more effective than a handful of pepper, at least they are easier to carry. Our own collection of these items includes everything from foreign-made metal containers dispensing a pleasant-smelling aerosol to domestic plastic tubes squirting a stream of foul odorous liquid. Before buying, look beyond the pretty container, and determine what is inside. Among features worth looking for are sprays which will *mark your opponent for future identification,* in addition to repelling him.

Because of possible permanent injury to the eyes with some of these chemicals, sale is either prohibited completely or restricted to persons over twenty-one years of age, in certain localities. We may be wrong, but offhand we cannot think of any law, rule, or ordinance that prohibits the possession of a leakproof water pistol, or other handy plastic squirt container, filled with indelible laundry ink. And wouldn't our psychological warfare friends be proud of us if they could hear our yell, "Watch that acid in your face," as we make use of this secret weapon.

Then there are guns. There are big ones and small ones, there are expensive models with fancy grips, and there are less luxurious models.

If you now own anything from heavy artillery to a small pea shooter, you are well aware of the grave responsibilities which go with owning a gun. If you are considering the purchase of a gun, give yourself an extra twenty-four hours to think about it; don't ever become the owner of a firearm on the spur of the moment.

Want to scare the neighbor's kids with this new weapon because they cut across your lawn again? Want to stop that infernal noise in the apartment above you once and for all? Impress the girl friend with it? Stop that bold boyfriend from kissing you good night? Could any of these be *the real reason* for your purchase, while rationalizing that it might also come in handy for self-defense? To buy a gun for any of the above reasons is as logical as marrying someone who owns a plane because you need a ride home from two blocks away. If that were not bad enough, remember that the responsibility does not end with the ride or purchase.

Best, by Far

Avoid incidents.

Avoid bodily contact.

Avoid trouble of any kind—it *can* be done!

There is such a thing as a completely unprovoked attack, but were you to know *all* the details preceding an attack reported as "unprovoked," you'd be surprised what you would find in over 90 percent of cases.

There was this stranger, Mr. Sharpy, who at four o'clock in the morning was still flirting with Toughy's girl, although the boys tried to warn drunken Sharpy of the boyfriend's return. There was Miss Dizzy, inspecting a slum area and minding her own business; except that it was dark and she still wore that $10,000 fur coat of hers. Of course, the fellow we saw display all those big bills in country "Z" never quite made it back to the hotel without getting an ever so slight dent in his head. Open your newspaper tomorrow morning and read about the three completely unprovoked (?) attacks on these three innocent (but oh, so careless!) citizens.

Cops are no different!

The most vivid, most startling, and most concrete evidence we ever heard to substantiate our theory about being able to avoid trouble came from a chief of police. He was not talking about you or me, he was talking about his own policemen, and had facts and figures handy to prove his point.

Neither the uniform of a cop, nor the fancy hat of a state trooper, nor the credentials of a federal agent can keep any of them from getting hurt or killed. For that reason a joint federal, state, and local meeting was called not very long ago. It was the chief's turn to speak. It seems that too many of his officers, operating prowl cars at night in tough areas alone, got wounded or even killed. To remedy this situation, he put two officers in each car, certainly considered a prudent move by most of us. Imagine his surprise when, over a period of time, the injury and death rate for his men *climbed* in those areas!

His simple, logical explanation: Any policeman alone will "stay on his toes" at all times, will use a proper amount of caution, and will summon help before doing anything recklessly. When there are two, neither wants to appear overly cautious and certainly will not stand for any ribbing back at the station house for being "chicken." Result: They must impress *each other,* and show their partner how brave they really are. It is not uncommon that the number two man gets shot with his own partner's gun, because number one dashed in without sufficient caution, was overpowered, and had his gun taken away. We are not talking about rookies, cadets, or beginners at this game, we are talking about well-disciplined, well-trained, and experienced police officers.

The above example was *not* given to rearrange any police department in the nation. It was *not* given to criticize the buddy system. It was given to show how even a capable police officer can throw caution to the wind in order to become a show-off. *If temptation to show off can affect a well-trained, seasoned officer—how much easier for you and me to succumb.*

What does all this mean? To many of us it means that no matter who you are, or what your position in life, it *is* possible to avoid trouble, at least to a large degree. For that reason we urge that you use caution, stay alert, and not become careless: *today, tomorrow, and always.*

-16-

Special Devices

If you were to die tomorrow of a disease for which we have not yet found a cure, your body could be frozen and would be brought back to life when the cure has been found. You already knew that. What you may not be aware of is that the discoverer of this process has no doubts about bringing you back to life successfully, but that he has expressed grave concern about the ever-increasing number of quacks with the door to a deepfreeze open, ready to cash in on a good deal.

The author has no doubt that security devices on the market today can keep you quite safe while your body temperature is still 98.6 degrees. What he is terribly concerned about is the growing number of fellows who were fired from their gas pumping job the day before yesterday, then tried to peddle encyclopedias for eight hours, and to-day want to high-pressure you into buying the most expensive device available, hoping you will also take all of the $1,000 worth of "extras." The one and only thing many of these characters know about security, or security devices, is how much commission each item puts into their wide-open hand.

Well-made, sophisticated, and effective devices, built by reputable manufacturers, can be advertised by any one of these unscrupulous fellows in such a manner and at such reasonable cost, that you can't resist his offer.

But wait!

Did he also tell you that this device *by itself* will do as much for the security of your home as an engine developing 465 horses with four-barrel carburetor will do *by itself* to solve your transportation problem? Without wheels, that powerful engine does not even take you to the local grocer. Without sensory devices, that particular instrument will just sit there and collect dust.

So you find out that these small sensory devices are needed to report an entry at one of your doors or windows to the master unit, which sounds the alarm, activates the phone, or whatever. You also determine the cost for each of these little gadgets, and are pleasantly surprised that they are not terribly expensive. The surprise becomes less pleasant when you multiply this price by the total number of windows and doors which are to be protected and find that Sharpy is ready to charge twice as much for these gadgets as the price advertised for the original unit. Still, it sounds like a good unit, so you order.

What about installation? Are they just going to dump everything on your living-room floor? That dealer may demand more money for installation alone than he asked for master unit and sensory devices combined. And even if you are willing to pay the price, are installers going to run wires right over your dining-room table, or will he make additional charges to hide all wires properly? If the high-pressure salesman knew nothing about the device which is totally unsuited for your purpose, that greasy handyman who follows may know even less about its proper installation.

Impossible? Then listen to the sad tale of two perfectly good and completely sound security devices which were both installed fairly recently in the Big City.

1. A large department store, well protected at night by guards and roving dogs, was sold a bill of goods about even better protection for their silverware and jewelry. An effective electronic device that detected any movement within these departments was installed. Certainly, you guessed it, the alarm went off every time the trained watchdogs made their rounds throughout the store.

2. A well-known nightclub (you have heard the name) closed its doors forever. Because of its fame, ample television coverage was given this event. As the commentator came to the end of his sorrowful saga, the camera moved in for a closeup of the new addition to

the entrance door: one of the largest padlocks you ever saw. The picture was so clear that this observer was able to judge the lock to be an effective, well-made, and probably quite expensive item. Just as clearly, just as detailed, were the four completely unprotected screws which held the hasp in place, inviting all those owning a screwdriver to bypass the lock and enter.

We cite these two examples (from a collection of hundreds) to prove how misuse through lack of understanding of the functions and capabilities of one device and improper installation of another can completely nullify their usefulness.

Wheelers and Dealers

Security devices *can* be helpful; surely I am not against them, and only wish to present here as objective and unbiased a professional opinion as I can offer. But before turning to the pros and cons of the specific devices themselves, let us briefly consider the people who offer these items for sale, or advise you about their proper use. Most are honest, reliable businessmen. Many are new to this relatively new business, but they make an honest effort to learn as much as possible about it. Much of the burden will rest on your own shoulders if you want to make certain that the device in question is the one best suited to your purpose. Ask detailed questions, and if something is still not quite clear in your mind, ask again, *before* signing any contract.

As for our discussion about the unscrupulous ones in this group—that was only a warning. You are fully aware of the practices of certain high-pressure car dealers, who only after the contract has been signed explain that the model on the floor has a "deluxe" steering wheel at $40 extra, and that the whitewalls would also add another $40 to the agreed price.

The big difference between the purchase of an automobile and the purchase of a burglar alarm lies in the fact that we have been *conditioned* to the practice of many automobile dealers who quote a price for the stripped model only, but what on earth constitutes a "stripped" model for a security device about which most people know nothing? More important: A car will run without fancy steering wheel or whitewalls, while many sophisticated security devices will do absolutely nothing without a certain number of essential "extras."

To make life easier for you and to help ask pertinent, intelligent questions about the device you may want to purchase, we added a checklist at the end of this book.

Apropos of purchase, the common practice of the automobile industry has never stopped us from buying another car; don't let excess caution keep you from buying a good, reliable security device.

Take Your Choice

No matter who wants to say what about which security device, the one thing none of us can possibly complain about is the vast variety of choice which hundreds of inventors and manufacturers have given us with the literally thousands of security items on the market today.

Over the years the author collected pounds and pounds of interesting literature at fairs, exhibits, and conferences, all describing new wares in the security field. With no claim to having the largest collection of its kind in the world, we have never had the pleasure of seeing a more extensive accumulation.

Don't get the idea that we looked only at flowery words and pretty pictures of new products; we made purchases to examine interesting items closely, we interrogated factory representatives, visited manufacturing plants, conducted many tests, and searched patent files in Washington, D.C. The one irrevocable finding: *Man did manage to make an improvement or two over the first rock that secured the entrance to a cave—even managed to improve on the caveman's club somewhat.*

Yet, if the rock guarding your entrance fits so perfectly that it affords adequate protection, by all means continue to use it. If that club you have carried for years never got too heavy, don't bother to look at expensive new gadgets for self-defense. Freely translated this means: Examine your present security items carefully. If you find them to be sturdy, reliable, and effective, then don't make changes merely for the sake of change. (Unlike automobile taillights, last year's device can be as fashionable today as it was yesterday.)

If, on the other hand, your present security setup has outlived its usefulness, has given you nothing but trouble, or shows gaps and loopholes big enough for a truck to pass through undetected, then it might be worth your while to take a closer look at some of the items listed here.

Hiding Places

When you consider the fact that all your uncles believe their wallet safe because they button that back pocket, all aunts consider a pocket-book safe because they clutch it tightly while standing under a "Warning, Pickpockets" sign (and five minutes later forget in which washroom they left it), you may want something more secure. Not while buying the morning paper, or while running over to the corner grocer for a container of milk, but while vacationing in some distant place with additional money and difficult-to-replace identification.

The old money belt, worn under your clothing around the waist, is still effective. But what woman in her right mind wants to add even one-quarter of an inch to her streamlined waist? Well, consider a just as old-fashioned garter, only this one with a small zippered pocket.

And there is a wallet on the market which, with a simple patented wire inside, will remain in the owner's pocket—even after long fingers have managed to reach an inside pocket which they unbuttoned.

Just as experienced thieves will expect to find a few bills of large denomination neatly folded in an out-of-towner's shoe, they will look for funds hidden on the third shelf of your linen closet. But a small metal box, which can be easily mounted in most unlikely places, like under the center of a dining-room table (you can think of much better locations) may well go undetected.

Even 300-pound safes have been removed from premises, so don't

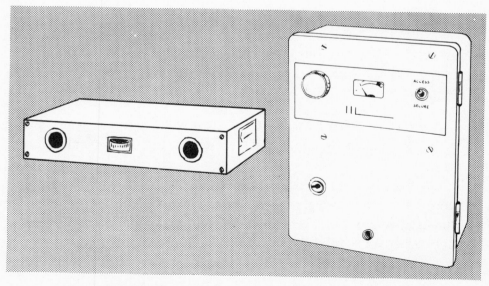

(Left) An ultrasonic motion detector can protect an entire area.
(Right) Or you can let this unit give the alarm when your safe is touched.

rely on your little box's good looks or sturdy lock alone. Find the craziest hiding place, then bolt it down as firmly as possible.

Square and cylindrical safes in all sizes are also available, ready to be mounted flush inside wall or floor. To make sure that container serves a dual purpose, ascertain that there is at least some insulation to protect valuables against fire.

Too much of value in there for comfort? Then add:

1. An electronic detector which will be activated by anyone who comes within so many feet (your guests could set it off if you don't keep it out of family traffic patterns, or else activate the unit only when retiring).

2. The device that sounds the alarm when the safe is touched (better keep the maid's dustrag away).

3. Or one which only sounds the alarm when the safe is being tampered with (you may find this a little late for appropriate action).

Afraid that an intruder may force you, or a member of your family, to open the safe? Then dial the combination or turn the proper key obligingly and point (with pride) to the large decal, announcing that a delaying device keeps the safe locked for whatever time it is set (and you thought that this delay was only available to your local banker). The fact that the nearest police precinct has been alerted through direct line in the meantime might be of possible interest to the intruder.

Open Sesame or Fun with the Garage Door

Many good devices are on the market to make it easier for the motorist to get safely into his garage. Before purchasing, consider the following:

1. A beam of light across your driveway to activate your garage door can be broken by anyone. This then would be convenience, not security.

2. Doors opened on a certain radio frequency from your car are fine, but make sure that the garage is not too near an airport, else check on the frequency used. We know of too many doors that open at strange hours on a pilot's request for landing instructions.

3. A rural type of mailbox, only much smaller, with a lock inside,

can be mounted anywhere along the driveway at car-window height. Turning the proper key in this lock will open the door.

4. Leave the car in the driveway, with the driving lights on, illuminating the front door. Go into your home, and let the delaying device, now available on certain cars, turn the lights off after so many seconds. The car? Put it in the garage tomorrow.

Door Locks

Again we say that this book was not written to help you spend money, or to imply that your present locks are worthless. However, if

1. You are about to build your own home,
2. You have just moved in and don't know how many keys are out,

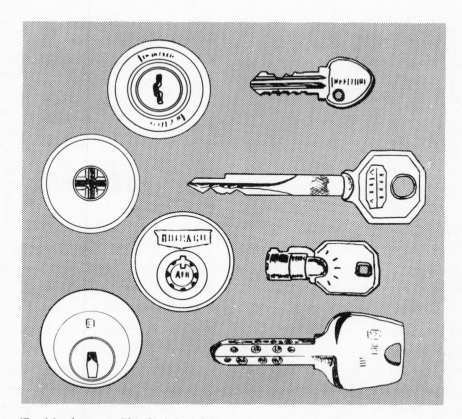

(Top) Lock types: This lock has five pins up and five pins down.
(Upper center) This one has three sets of pins in three directions.
(Lower center) This one has pins arranged in a circle.
(Bottom) Here three sets of pins huddle in a tight formation.

3. You know that one of your keys is in the "wrong" hands,

4. The lock no longer operates properly,

and you plan to buy new locks anyway, then be advised that you can get more than just another identical replacement. Let your local locksmith explain how the extra dollar spent on a better lock will pay big dividends in peace of mind.

The chances are excellent that you neither have to buy a new door, nor a new locking mechanism, in order to get better protection. Standardization makes everything simpler. Just as your electric hair dryer or shaver will fit any outlet in Wichita, Kansas, or Lake George, New York, the new lock will fit well into the existing threaded cylinder of your present door. Any locksmith can perform this operation in seconds. If you plan to do it yourself, please take an extra few minutes to read the accompanying instructions carefully.

Standardization is a wonderful thing. But what about the design or pattern that is everywhere repeated? As a nation we carry the identical flat key for home, for car, for office, and just about everything else. Is its pattern worthy of this uniform use?

A ridge, slightly deeper cut on your key, prevents its entering your neighbor's door, but the four or five little pins inside the lock are arranged in the same manner, and work on the same principle. It follows then that the same tension bar, rake, diamond, vibration gun, or other simpler burglar tool is as effective in Wichita as it is in Lake George. But there are locks with *ten* pins, five up, five down. There are locks with *three* series of pins, spaced in the three, six, and nine o'clock position on your watch. There are locks with pins arranged in a *circle* instead of one straight row, and then there are completely *keyless* locks.

One of the most recent additions to the lock family has the pins arranged in such a manner that insertion of anything but the proper key is almost impossible. This is not only a superior lock, but one that is not weakened by masterkeying, described in Chapter 11 as so dangerous. Change here, as well as in the following lock, can be accomplished in the *key,* without disturbing lock security.

Although the first magnetic lock was patented in 1892, many changes had to be made to produce what evolved as an effective lock. A perfectly smooth cyclindrical keyway receives perfectly round and smooth key. Tiny magnets spaced inside each do the work. While shopping for locks, you may want to look at the new types of latches. Locking

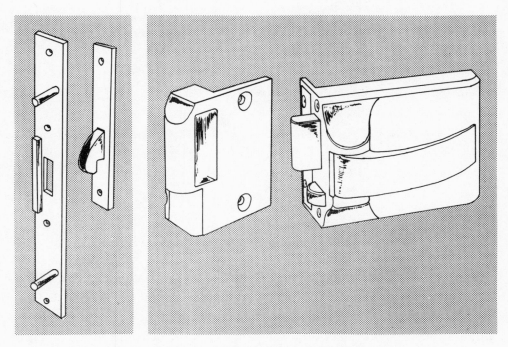

Some new bolts, latches, and lock strikes with built-in protection.

guard and/or new shapes will make them completely safe not only against that overused laminated credit card but also the most professional shove knife.

Have you seen any of these locks or latches lately? Probably not. All those we inspected were good and well made—but none has become what might be called "popular." Not because they don't offer much better security, but they cost an extra dollar or two which we are not willing to spend.

Closed Circuit Television

Proper application and operation of closed circuit TV can actually save money on security for large establishments, although because of its cost this method will probably not be used in most homes for some time.

Mounting brackets for cameras make it possible to place them anywhere; special housings (complete with windshield wiper) make it possible to protect them outdoors from July sun to December hailstorms. They can remain stationary, oscillate, or be aimed from a

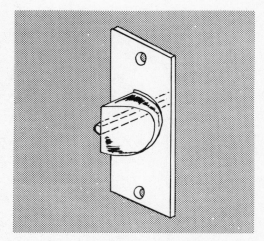

A modern latch-guard prevents unauthorized opening.

control panel. They come as empty shells, for psychological effect only, or can be outfitted with the most outlandish remote-controlled lenses. Receivers give instant picture, or movies can be taken for future showing and positive identification. Consoles make it possible for one guard or doorman to monitor several cameras.

Now a camera can be mounted at the entrance of any apartment building, and has only to be wired to one master antenna. Instead of answering the doorbell from Apt. 123 with a buzz, Mrs. O'Toole turns *her present TV set* to channel X (channel not used for broadcast in her area) and gets beautiful reception from the camera downstairs.

Self-Contained Alarms

No extras to buy.
No wires to string.
No big expense involved.
Sounds as though this is just the type of unit you had in mind?

Available in easy-to-mount housings ranging in size from a large pack of cigarettes to Dad's cigar box, made of material that ranges from beer can thickness (thinness) to sturdy, lockable steel boxes. When the alarms go off, some sound like a sick refrigerator motor, others like the alarm clock next to your bed, or the type of annoying loud noise made by certain new emergency vehicles. The alarm may be powered

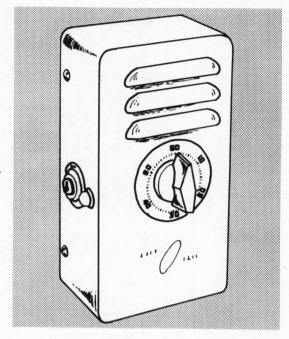

A self-contained alarm.

by batteries, 110-volt house current, a mechanical windup spring, or a combination of these. Before buying, make sure that this is the type of unit for you, since it must be mounted at the point of possible entry.

Small apartment on the twelfth floor, with no fire escape window and only one entrance door to protect, fine! But you may not live on the twelfth floor. Perhaps you own an impressive big home on beautiful grounds in the right section of suburbia. You have spent money on alarms—have one here, there, everywhere. There's one in the basement, too, although you can't possibly detect an alarm going off three flights below your pillow, at the other end of the mansion.

Alarm Systems

Or perhaps you do not live in a mansion, but may have more than one door to guard. In that case we strongly urge you to check into a system requiring but one master unit, which can be instructed by various and sundry sensory devices to do just about anything under the sun for you.

In its simplest form, the system consists of something similar to the self-contained alarm described above, but a low-current bell wire connects the alarm to inexpensive sensors, guarding all your windows and doors. Not only can you save money by purchasing a single master unit, but the alarm itself can be mounted wherever desired. This includes the headboard above your pillow.

This is the same type of unit we cautioned you about earlier, which will do nothing without sensory devices. A few examples of the hundreds of sensors available and what they can do for you:

1. Report person entering your driveway, or on your property.
2. Report breaking and entering, but before this happens caution you about any window or door not properly secured.
3. Report person in wine cellar, where you never want anybody to go.
4. Warn of deepfreeze getting too warm, or greenhouse getting too cold.
5. Report fire, anywhere in house or garage.

You don't want a noisy alarm to go off just to announce that food may spoil in the deepfreeze? Then pick a red warning light or a pleasant glockenspiel playing your favorite tune to announce this event.

But you may not be home when something happens to your house. Then let a loud outside noisemaker announce to neighbors that the house is in difficulties. No neighbors? Let direct lines to police and fire departments give the alarm, or get a unit that will give a recorded message *via your present telephone* to police to report an entry, a different taped message to the fire department to report a fire, and a third to the utility company in case of major appliance trouble. Not only that, any of these reports can be followed by two more calls of your choice, such as one to your summer home, another to your trusted friend nearby. Sensing, distinguishing between emergencies, dialing the phone, giving a proper report to include address to parties concerned—all automatic.

Because of a possible ailment you might be much more concerned about yourself than about steaks spoiling inside a big white box. In that case, have your unit set so that it will dial your doctor, then your husband at the office, and maybe the next door neighbor (or whomever you want to notify that you had another attack and need help). How will the machine know when to start dialing these numbers? As soon as you push a button on the easy-to-carry radio transmitter that you can have on your person at all times, since it is identical in size to a pack of cigarettes. The transmitter will not only work from anywhere in your home, but also from that shady tree, where the doctor told you to sit and get some rest.

No, not every home needs every "extra." But knowing what is available, you may want to question the alarm system salesman if an extra you plan to add at some future date is available and compatible with the master unit he is about to sell you.

Don't Ever Cry Wolf

There are some cheap, self-contained alarms on the market which can only be activated from *inside* the house, and should be used only after the last member of the household is home, since they will go off for burglar and returning owner alike.

Most self-contained alarms and some alarm systems have a built-in delay before sounding the alarm, allowing the returning owner to enter and within a few seconds break the alarm cycle with the proper key, preventing the unit from going off. Some systems have a key-operated switch outside, allowing you to enter at your leisure and reset the alarm from the inside control. No matter which unit you now own or plan to purchase at some future date, make sure that it does not cry wolf when there is not even a pussy cat in the vicinity!

Neighbors, police, and firemen, no matter how cheerful and helpful, will soon slow their pace when responding to your alarm if it has brought them too often to your home unnecessarily. Improper handling of the unit, improper installation, or plain carelessness can be responsible for a false alarm in the very best of systems.

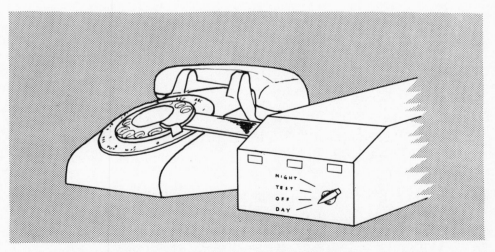

A small unit can make emergency calls automatically, yet does not interfere with the ordinary use of your phone.

Checklists

Before Retiring at Night

DOORS   Are they secured properly, not just shut?

WINDOWS   Closed? Locked? If partially open, make sure the lock or alarm is in the correct position.

KEYS   Are all keys in the proper place near those doors and windows which are secured with key locks from the inside (so that a hasty exit can be effected in case of emergency)? Are any keys left in the lock on the outside of the door (by someone carrying too many packages to retract the key on the way in)? Is the key removed from the car ignition? Is the key removed from the burglar alarm outside shutoff?

VALUABLES   Are they locked or hidden in their proper places?

ALARM   Is it armed (turned on) and functioning properly?

WEAPON   Is it in a handy, yet safe, place?

LIGHTS   Are the show-off lights turned off? Are the security lights on and functioning properly?

TELEPHONE   Does the dial tone assure you that the line is in order, especially if the alarm system utilizes this line?

HEADCOUNT   Are all occupants present, including Rover, so the night latch or chain can be locked?

Good night!

Before Buying an Alarm System

SUITABILITY   The best outside visual or audio alarm will not be very effective if nearest neighbor is miles away. Consider a system that notifies the police, fire department, or answering service directly. The best area sensor becomes useless if roving Rover sets off a false alarm periodically.

DEPENDABILITY   What do you know about the salesman, dealer, or name on the equipment? Call the Better Business Bureau, your bank, or check with persons where equipment has already been installed.

RELIABILITY   Does the equipment look flimsy? Homemade? Are you buying the first, untested prototype?

SIMPLICITY   Does a complicated control panel require an engineering degree? Can one prominent master switch be operated easily by Junior, when he returns late at night?

VERSATILITY   Can it announce only breaking and entering? Can fire sensors be added for a few extra dollars?

SENSITIVITY   A salesman may point out proudly that the vibration contacts or other sensory devices in his system are so delicate that the slightest touch or vibration will set off the alarm. Make sure that these devices are adjustable to *less* sensitivity, so that a rumbling truck outside or Junior's drums inside will no longer activate your new alarm.

COMPATABILITY   Can the existing fire alarm be connected to this new unit? Are sophisticated sensors, which you may want to add in the future, available for this system or do you have to buy an entire new master unit?

FEES   Will this be an outright purchase, or will there be a monthly rental fee for equipment and/or lines to the police, fire department, guard service, or whatever.

RESPONSE   Will a high monthly charge of $50 to $100 assure you of a well-trained, armed, and uniformed guard in a radio car at your home within seconds? Some services, with the above monthly charge, maintain only one individual on night watch at their office. In case of an emergency in your home, he calls the police, and that is the extent of his duties.

POLICE   In some communities police have a board with dozens of addresses mounted in their headquarters, precinct, or station house. In case an alarm goes off at any of these locations, a small red bulb lights up alongside this address, and the nearest radio car is dispatched by the officer on duty. Because of limited facilities, this board may be available only to commercial plants, and because of financial restrictions it cannot be expanded by the police department. Check with your civic organization or neighbors; buying such a board for the department may be cheaper in the long run than paying the above-mentioned monthly charges, and will certainly save considerable time in getting police response in an emergency.

GUARANTEE   Is the entire system guaranteed in writing for a certain length of time? If not, how high is the maintenance fee, and what does it entail?

TESTS   A good system can be checked by you anytime, then resets itself and is ready for use. Cheap equipment, like certain fire sensors, operate only once, then must be replaced.

VENTILATION   Do you want fresh air? Make sure the system is effective with partially open windows. This is easily done with a sensor mounted several inches above the windowsill, but impossible to achieve with certain alarms.

FALSE ALARM   Good equipment will allow the owner to enter the premises without sounding an alarm. A delaying device makes it possible for the owner to enter, shut off the system with the proper key from inside, and then reset it. Make certain that the time lapse is sufficient for all members of household.

SHUT-OFF   A switch, mounted outside the home, and operated with the proper key, will allow as much time as needed to enter a protected dwelling. However, this method can nullify an entire $1,000 system if the cheapest lock available is used in this vulnerable spot.

ANTIPICK   Attempts at picking locks can be made extremely difficult simply by installing a lock above eye level. Especially outside, shut-off switches should be mounted at a height where the homeowner can comfortably reach to insert the proper key.

TYPES   There are two basic principles involved in all alarm systems that utilize sensors connected with wires. "Arming" or turning on one type means letting a continuous flow of current run through the entire system. Not only sensors will set off this alarm, but the cutting of wires as well. The other kind depends on closing the circuit to give the alarm. In this latter system it is particularly important to hide or protect all wires and sensory devices as much as possible. Find out which one you are being offered.

TELEPHONE   Make sure that the system is approved by the telephone company if it utilizes your present phone line. You may not only lose the use of the alarm, but regular telephone service as well.

POWER   Will a battery take over during electricity failure?

COST   A simple yet effective system does not have to cost very much. If you want something more elaborate and sophisticated, this can run into real money. However, a home improvement loan or inclusion into the mortgage for a new house can soften this blow considerably.